Teach Me
SPORTS
BASKETBALL

By Barry Dreayer

D0981551

Updated Edition

General Publishing Group, Inc.
Los Angeles

Publisher: W. Quay Hays
Editor: Barry Dreayer
Managing Editor: Colby Allerton
Cover Design: Kurt Wahlner
Production Director: Nadeen Torio
Production Assistant: Catherine Bailey
Copy Editor: Charles Neighbors

Special thanks to the following individuals for their
assistance with The Basketball Edition: Pete Babcock,
Vicki Blumenfeld, John Chymczuk, John Gabriel, Paul Joffe,
Darrin May, Wally Rooney, Evan Silverman.

All views and opinions expressed herein are solely those of
the author.

The *Teach Me Sports*™ series is published by
General Publishing Group, Inc., 2701 Ocean Park Blvd.,
Suite #140, Santa Monica, CA 90405, 310-314-4000.

Library of Congress Catalog Number 94-078815
ISBN 1-881649-33-4

10 9 8 7 6 5 4 3 2

Printed in the USA by RR Donnelley & Sons

INTRODUCTION

Since there are only 5 players on the court at one time for each team, basketball is a sport that is not overwhelming to the novice fan. However, the numerous infractions—violations, personal fouls and technical fouls—make it frustrating for those who do not closely follow the game. *Teach Me Sports Basketball* explains and illustrates these infractions along with the strategy, terminology, scoring and statistics that are a part of basketball.

This book begins with the assumption that the reader is aware that basketball involves "players wearing uniforms who dribble the ball, pass the ball and throw the ball into a hanging basket." From this basic premise, the book presents a crash course on becoming an educated basketball fan. It is meant to be used while watching the games on TV and/or in person.

Teach Me Sports Basketball is based on the professional game played by the National Basketball Association (NBA). Separate sections are devoted to how college basketball differs.

The book does not attempt to cover every one of basketball's hundreds of rules and situations, and many examples have been simplified for the sake of clarity. The text shows the WHY behind the WHAT. (For example: Why a player might intentionally foul an opponent late in the game.)

So, come on and join the fun by learning the game!

Teach Me SPORTS
JOIN THE FUN BY LEARNING THE GAME

THE BASKETBALL EDITION

THE ORIGIN OF BASKETBALL

Dr. James Naismith faced a problem in December, 1891. While working as a physical education instructor at the Springfield, Massachusetts, YMCA, this Presbyterian minister was assigned the task of developing a way to keep men in shape indoors between football and baseball seasons. The existing program of calisthenics and gymnastics was too boring.

Naismith's solution? He asked the custodian to find two large boxes because he had devised a game that involved throwing a soccer ball into a box that hung from the balcony at each end of the gymnasium. (How does "boxball" sound?) The custodian could only find a couple of peach baskets, so they were used. After each score, a person on a ladder retrieved the ball from inside the basket.

In 1895, iron baskets with braided netting were developed. A long-hanging cord could be pulled by the referee, lifting the net, causing the ball to roll out. The "ball-fetcher" was no longer needed. In 1912, open-bottom baskets were first used. What took them so long?

Overzealous spectators often sat in the balcony close to one of the peach baskets and used broomsticks, umbrellas and their hands to interfere with balls shot toward the basket. To prevent fan interference, the baskets were attached to backboards.

Originally, there were nine men on the court for each team. Some teams agreed to play each other with up to fifty players on the court at the same time. Fans and players complained they lost sight of the ball in such a large crowd. In 1897, the number of players was reduced to five to emphasize speed instead of brute strength.

Over the next century, basketball has evolved into the modern-day version enjoyed by millions.

BASIC RULES AND OBJECTIVES

The primary objective is to score more points than the opposing team. There are three different ways to score:

- Two-point FIELD GOAL or BASKET — A player throws the ball into his basket from inside the THREE-POINT-LINE (discussed in detail later) during the action of the game.
- Three-point FIELD GOAL or BASKET — A player throws the ball into his basket from outside the three-point line during the action of the game.
- One-point FREE THROW — A player throws the ball into his basket from 15 feet away while there is an official stop in the action.
  - Free throw attempts take place when the opposing team is guilty of certain rule infractions (discussed in detail later).

Each team is allowed 5 players on the court at one time.

- OFFENSE — When the team has possession of the basketball.
- DEFENSE — When the team does not have possession of the basketball.

There are 48 minutes of play divided into two 24-minute HALVES. HALFTIME is a 15-minute intermission that takes place between each half of play.

- Each half is divided into two 12-minute QUARTERS (or PERIODS).
- If teams are tied after 48 minutes, they play another five minutes, called an OVERTIME PERIOD.
  - If teams are still tied, they play as many additional overtime periods as needed until there is a winner.
- If a successful field goal attempt occurs just before the end of the period, but time expires while the ball is in the air, the points count.
  - For the points to count the ball must be released by the shooter before the clock shows that no time was remaining in the period.

*Former coach Bill van Breda Kolff
was asked why he preferred coaching
women's basketball. He replied:
"The timeouts smell better."*

- Time stops during a game when:
    - There is a DEAD BALL as a result of the following:
        1. PERSONAL FOUL or TECHNICAL FOUL (discussed in detail later).
        2. Two players on opposing teams simultaneously hold the basketball (called a HELD BALL).
        3. VIOLATION — A player breaks one of the rules such as "walking" with the ball without bouncing it (discussed in detail later).
        4. The end of each period.
    - A field goal attempt is successful in the last minute of the first three quarters and in the last two minutes of the fourth quarter (or an overtime period).
    - TEAM TIMEOUT — A team may choose to stop the clock when it has possession of the ball or there is a dead ball.
        1. Here are some reasons why a team takes a team timeout:
            a. Make substitutions.
            b. Discuss strategy.
            c. Halt the opposing team's momentum.
            d. ICE THE SHOOTER
                - When an opposing player is about to attempt an important free throw in the last minute of a game, a timeout by the defense forces the shooter to have more time to think about the pressure of the free throw, with the intention of making him freeze up and miss his shot.
            e. MIDCOURT INBOUND OPTION (discussed in detail later).
        2. Each team is allowed one 20-SECOND TIMEOUT in each half.
            a. An unused 20-second timeout from the first half cannot be used in the second half.

Look for mandatory timeouts to be called once the scoreboard clock ticks down to the below two times in a quarter when subsequently there is a dead ball.

$$\boxed{6:59}$$

Over 5 minutes of the 12-minute quarter has elapsed

$$\boxed{2:59}$$

Over 9 minutes of the 12-minute quarter has elapsed

b. All overtime periods are considered part of the second half with regard to the 20-second timeout. If a 20-second timeout has already been called by a team in the third or fourth quarter, that team may not request another one in an overtime period.

c. Only one player on a team may be replaced during a 20-second timeout. If the team that called the timeout does not make a substitution, the opposing team cannot make a substitution.

d. A player may yell, "twenty-second timeout" when requesting it.

   – Some players tap the top of their shoulders to signal for a 20-second timeout. When an official acknowledges the request, he also taps the top of his shoulders.

e. Any guesses as to the length of a 20-second timeout?

3. Each team is allowed to call up to seven REGULAR TIMEOUTS during the four quarters. Three regular timeouts may be called by each team in an overtime period regardless how many timeouts were used during the four quarters.

a. Two regular timeouts must be called in each quarter (so that broadcasted games will be guaranteed at least two opportunities to air commercials during each quarter).

   – If a regular timeout has not been called by either team in the first 5 minutes of a quarter, the HOME TEAM will be charged with a MANDATORY TIMEOUT after the next dead ball situation.

   – If a second regular timeout has not been called in the first 9

How Does Each Period Begin?

1st Period — Jump Ball

2nd Period — Team that did not control 1st period jump ball inbounds ball.

3rd Period — Same as 2nd period.

4th Period — Team that did control 1st period jump ball inbounds ball.

Each Overtime Period — Jump Ball

minutes of a quarter, the team that does not yet have a timeout in that quarter will be charged with a mandatory timeout after the next dead ball situation.

- Most basketball fans are not aware of these mandatory time-out rules. (You can have some fun at a basketball game by "boldly predicting" the next timeout when you are sure a team is due for a mandatory.)

b. Each team is only allowed four regular timeouts in the fourth quarter, and only three regular timeouts in the last 2 minutes of the fourth.

c. Regular timeouts are normally 100 seconds long.

The VISITING TEAM chooses its basket for the first half.

- Teams switch baskets between the first and second halves.

If a player is replaced by a substitute, he is allowed to return to the game.

- A substitution can only take place when there is a dead ball.

The game begins with a JUMP BALL at the middle of the court in the CENTER CIRCLE.

- An official tosses the ball into the air between a player designated by each team.
  - The two players involved try to tap the ball to one of their surrounding teammates.
  - The two players can only tap the ball when it has reached the height of the toss, or on its way down. They cannot touch the ball as it rises.
  - The two players cannot catch the ball unless it touches the floor, the basket, the backboard or one of the other eight players.
  - The two designated players cannot tap the ball more than twice on a jump ball.

When George Raveling coached at Washington State University he made this interesting comment regarding his players' passing skills: "Fans never fall asleep at our games because they're afraid they might get hit with a pass."

- If the ball tossed by the official touches the floor without being tapped by one of the two players, play stops and there is another jump ball.
- The other eight players must stand outside of the center circle.
    1. Teammates may not stand next to each other if an opponent wants to stand between them.
- The team that gains possession after the jump ball also earns the privilege of throwing in the ball from OUT-OF-BOUNDS (outside the playing area) to begin the fourth quarter. The opposing team starts the second and third quarters by throwing in the ball from out-of-bounds, called INBOUNDING.
    1. Only the first quarter and each overtime period begin with a jump ball.

The team with possession of the ball tries to advance the ball to an area where it can throw (called SHOOT) the ball into its basket for a field goal.

- A player may advance the ball by throwing it to a teammate, called PASSING.
- A player may advance the ball by DRIBBLING, which is bouncing the ball with one hand. Once a player stops dribbling, he may not dribble again until the ball leaves his possession, either:
    - Voluntarily, such as passing the ball, or
    - Involuntarily, such as an opponent slapping the ball away.

After a team scores, the opposing team takes possession of the basketball out-of-bounds underneath its opponent's basket and inbounds the ball.

- An exception is the MIDCOURT INBOUND OPTION — If a team calls a regular timeout immediately upon gaining possession of the basketball during the last 2 minutes of the fourth quarter (or overtime) it may elect to restart the action out-of-bounds at the center of the court.
    - In the last 2 minutes of the game, if a player inbounds the ball after an opponent's

Until 1937, after a team scored there used to be a jump ball. This slowed the game down too much and gave an unfair advantage to a team with a tall player who could easily WIN THE TAP.

successful field goal attempt and then calls a regular timeout, it is too late. He has given up the midcourt inbound option by advancing the ball *before* calling for a timeout.

- In the last 2 minutes of the game, if a player gains possession of an opponent's missed shot and either dribbles the ball or passes it and then requests a regular timeout, he gives up the midcourt inbound option. The timeout must be requested before advancing or dribbling the ball.
- The midcourt inbound option is not available if a team immediately requests a *20-second* timeout (instead of a *regular* timeout) upon gaining possession.
- The purpose of the midcourt inbound option is to make it easier for a team to try to win or tie a game even though the opponent has just tied or taken the lead with a few seconds left. The trailing team does not have to spend valuable time moving the ball to the center of the court.

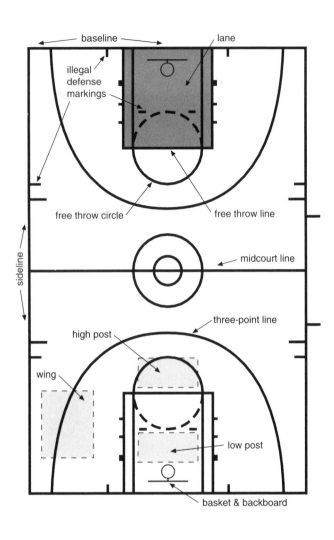

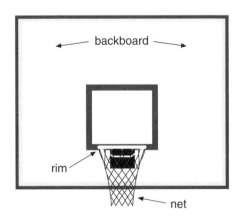

THE BASKETBALL COURT

The court is 94 feet long and 50 feet wide.

The line at each end of the court is called the BASELINE or ENDLINE.

The SIDELINES border the length of the court from one baseline to another.

When the ball or a player with possession of the ball touches a sideline, baseline or beyond those lines, the team whose player touched the ball last loses possession of the ball.

- The opposing team takes possession of the ball at the place where the ball went out-of-bounds.
    - If the ball is inbounded, does not touch a player, and goes out-of-bounds, the opposing team takes possession of the ball at the place where the ball was inbounded.
    - At an official's signal, a stationary player on the opposing team, standing out-of-bounds, tries to inbound the ball to a teammate.

Each BASKET is 10 feet above the court and is attached to a rectangular BACKBOARD (sometimes called the WINDOW or GLASS because most are transparent).

- A basket consists of the RIM and the NET that a ball must pass through (from above) to count as a score.
- Other terms for the basket or the rim include: HOOP, BUCKET, GOAL, RACK and RING.
- The basket where a team shoots to score is its own basket.
    - The half of the court that includes a team's basket is that team's FRONTCOURT.
    - The other half of the court is that team's BACKCOURT. A team's backcourt also includes the MIDCOURT LINE dividing the court.
- Except for the rear of the backboard, all other parts of it are considered inbounds.

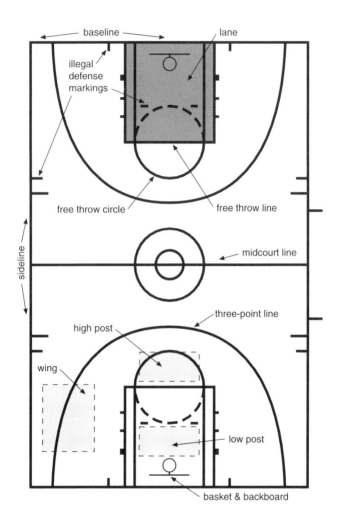

baseline

lane

illegal defense markings

free throw circle

free throw line

sideline

midcourt line

three-point line

high post

wing

low post

basket & backboard

      – Some fans mistakenly believe that the top or the side of the backboard is out-of-bounds, too.

The FREE THROW LINE is 15 feet from the backboard.

- Players shooting free throws may not step on or over the free throw line until the ball touches the rim or backboard.
- A FREE THROW CIRCLE surrounds each free throw line.

The rectangular area of the court from the free throw line to the baseline is called the LANE or KEY.

    The THREE-POINT LINE is an arc from one side of the baseline to the other, at a distance between 22 feet and 23 feet, 9 inches from the center of the basket.

- If both of a player's feet are behind the three-point line before he shoots the ball, three points are awarded if the ball goes in the basket.
- If a player's foot is on the three-point line or in front of the line just before he shoots the ball, only two points are awarded if the ball goes in the basket.

Many markings on the floor are used to help enforce the ILLEGAL DEFENSE rules (discussed in detail later).

HIGH POST — The area near each FREE THROW CIRCLE.

LOW POST — The area near each basket. Sometimes the low post is referred to as the BLOCK.

WINGS — The area between the lane and each sideline.

Al McGuire, current broadcaster and former coach and player, once used the following analogy to describe the importance of the point guard to a team:

"If you cut the head off, you kill the body."

In other words, if you defend the opponent's point guard effectively so he is not as productive and makes mistakes, that opponent will most likely lose.

THE PLAYERS

BACKCOURT — The two players (GUARDS) who position themselves farthest from the basket.

- POINT GUARD
    - Primary responsibility is to distribute the ball to his teammates so they can score.
    - Usually dribbles the ball from his backcourt to his frontcourt to give his teammates time to position themselves to receive a pass.
    - Many consider the point guard the most important player on the team.
        1. Handles the ball more than any other player.
        2. Many times is referred to as the "quarterback" of the team.
    - Usually between 6 feet and 6 feet 5 inches tall.
        1. Point guards are normally shorter than other players. While dribbling, the ball has a shorter distance to travel between the court and a shorter point guard's hand—minimizing the opportunity of an opponent to steal the ball.
        2. Some point guards do not fall within this height range.
            a. Most notably, the great former point guard with the Los Angeles Lakers, Earvin "Magic" Johnson. He was a 6-feet-9-inches tall point guard.
            b. Tyrone "Muggsy" Bogues's career has almost been entirely with the Charlotte Hornets as their 5-feet-3-inches tall point guard.
    - Other names for this position are PLAYMAKING GUARD, LEAD GUARD or POINT.

- SHOOTING GUARD
    - Primary responsibility is to shoot the basketball, but may at times act as a point guard in dribbling and distributing the ball.

Former coach, Weldon Drew,
summarized his forwards as follows:
"We have a great bunch of outside
shooters. Unfortunately, all our
games are played indoors."

- Usually between 6 feet 3 inches and 6 feet 7 inches tall.
- The most famous shooting guard in the history of basketball is Michael Jordan, whose career was spent entirely with the Chicago Bulls.
- Other names for this position are OFF GUARD or TWO GUARD.

FRONTCOURT — The three players (two FORWARDS and one CENTER) who position themselves closer to the basket than the backcourt players.

- SMALL FORWARD
    - Primary responsibility is to shoot the basketball.
    - If a small forward can dribble effectively, he will sometimes play the shooting guard position.
    - Not only an accurate shooter from the PERIMETER (or OUTSIDE, 15 to 25 feet from the basket) but also scores frequently INSIDE or close to the basket.
    - Usually between 6 feet 6 inches and 6 feet 10 inches tall.
    - Another name for this position is SHOOTING FORWARD.
- POWER FORWARD
    - Primary responsibility is to REBOUND, which means gaining possession of a missed shot.
        1. OFFENSIVE REBOUND — Regain possession of the ball after a *teammate's* missed shot (including the rebounder's own missed shot).
        2. DEFENSIVE REBOUND — Gain possession of the ball after an *opponent's* missed shot.
    - Not as quick as the small forward but more powerful. He CRASHES THE BOARDS (aggressively jumps near the backboard) for rebounds.
    - In most cases, will not score as often as the small forward.
    - Usually between 6 feet 9 inches and 7 feet tall.
    - Another name for this position is BIG FORWARD.

Former New York Knicks center, Marvin Webster, had a fitting nickname— the Human Eraser. Webster was over seven feet tall and used to "wipe out" the field goal attempts of opponents by blocking their shots.

- **CENTER**
  - Primary responsibility is to intimidate the opposition with his height, mainly by BLOCKING SHOTS, which means deflecting a ball shot toward the opponent's basket.

    1. A shot may only be blocked as it is going up in its path to the basket. If the ball is in its downward arc to the basket when blocked, GOALTENDING will be called.

       a. On a goaltending call, two or three points are awarded to the shooting team (depending on where the shot originated—behind or in front of the three-point line).

       b. Goaltending is also called when a player touches a field goal attempt after the ball touches the backboard or if a player touches the ball with his hand through the net.

          - If a player TRAPS the ball against the backboard (the defender's hand, the ball and the backboard all touch at the same time) goaltending will be called.

          - If a player slaps the ball against the backboard, goaltending will not be called (unless the ball was on its downward path). It will not be treated as a trapped ball.

       c. For goaltending to be called, an official must believe the ball had a chance to go through the basket before it was touched.

    2. A shot may not be touched when the ball is within an imaginary cylinder rising above the rim, with the base the same circumference as the rim. This is called BASKET INTERFERENCE.

       a. Basket does not count and possession

Elmore Smith, the former center with the Los Angeles Lakers, looked like a fly swatter in his team's game against the Portland Trailblazers on October 28, 1973. Seventeen times during the game, Smith blocked a field goal attempt, to set an NBA record. (The statistic for blocked shots was first kept in 1973.)

goes to the opponents if an offensive player is guilty of basket interference.

    b. If a defender is called for basket interference, the offensive team earns two or three points (depending on where the shot originated—behind or in front of the three-point line).

– Usually the tallest players on a team.

– Most time spent in the low post to take advantage of their height for rebounding, blocking shots and shooting.

– Usually between 6 feet 10 inches and 7 feet 4 inches tall.

– Another name for this position is the PIVOT.

*Missing a dunk shot is embarrassing
to the shooter because he is so close to
the basket. It is also frustrating to his
coach who wanted points for his team
that could have easily been scored with a
layup. But why would a referee care if
a player missed a dunk shot?*

*On January 19, 1977, University of
Cincinnati guard, Brian Williams, gritted
his teeth and jumped toward the basket
for a slam dunk to inspire his teammates.
He missed…the rim, the backboard,
everything except the head of referee
Darwin Brown. The ball smashed into
Brown's head and went out-of-bounds.*

*We can assume that Williams was
a bit more careful during his next
slam dunk attempt.*

TERMS AND DEFINITIONS

SHOT — Attempt to score by throwing (shooting) the ball toward the basket.

- LAYUP — An easy shot taken right in front of or to the side of the basket. Many times a layup is BANKED off the backboard.

- JUMP SHOT or JUMPER — A player with possession of the ball jumps, shooting the ball when he has reached the height of his jump.

    - The most common type of shot in basketball.

    - If a player has an accurate jump shot, he is said to have a good "J."

- HOOK SHOT — A high arcing shot delivered over-head with one hand, usually taken by the center with his side facing the basket.

    - The player jumps off one foot, the one opposite his shooting hand, and shoots the ball with a high sweeping motion of his arm.

        1. Very difficult for a defender to block because the shooter of the hook shot is putting his body between the defender and the ball.

        2. If a player jumps off both feet when attempting a hook shot, it is called a JUMP HOOK.

- SET SHOT — A player shoots the ball with both feet on the floor. Very rarely used because it is so easy to block. More common in the early years of basketball.

- FINGER ROLL — A player jumps toward the basket with his "shooting" palm up and flicks the ball with his outstretched fingertips into the basket.

    - Former great center, Wilt Chamberlain, was famous for his finger roll.

- DUNK — A player jumps and slams the ball through the goal.

    - Also referred to as a JAM, SLAM or SLAM DUNK.

    - The most exciting, crowd-pleasing shot.

        1. A visiting coach frequently calls a

Scott Skiles was his teammates' best friend on December 30, 1990. While playing point guard for the Orlando Magic against the Denver Nuggets, Skiles set an NBA record—30 assists during the game. That means at least 60 points (30 assists x 2 points, not counting 3-point field goals) were scored by the Magic because of Skiles' passing.

Skiles' performance illustrates that a player can help a team's scoring without shooting the ball.

timeout after a home team's player dunks the ball to quiet the crowd and stop the momentum.

– Dunking has developed into an art. Many promotional basketball events include a slam dunk contest where players are judged on the style and difficulty of their dunk shots.

PASS — A way to get the ball to a teammate.

- CHEST PASS — Thrown with both hands pushing out from the chest.
- BOUNCE PASS — Thrown to a teammate with the ball hitting the floor once before it is caught.

    – Since most defenders expect to see a chest pass, the element of surprise increases the effectiveness of the bounce pass.

- BASEBALL PASS — A long pass thrown with one hand, usually from a player's backcourt to a teammate running toward his team's basket.
- OVERHEAD PASS — Thrown with both hands over his head, usually when a player is throwing the ball into play from the baseline or sideline.
- NO-LOOK PASS — A player looks in one direction and passes in another direction to a teammate who is preparing to shoot.

    – The "fancy" no-look pass is sometimes called FRENCH PASTRY.

    – Magic Johnson, the former point guard with the Los Angeles Lakers, was the "king" of the no-look passers.

ASSIST — A pass that leads directly to a score. Once the receiver of the pass catches the ball, he must immediately begin the process of shooting a successful field goal attempt for the passer to receive credit for the assist.

DRIVE — Moving quickly toward the basket while dribbling. Frequently, a broadcaster describes it as DRIVING TO THE HOOP.

PENETRATE THE DEFENSE — A player, usually a guard,

*Air balls are understandable
when a player attempts a field goal
from the wing while being closely
guarded by an opponent. But, while
attempting a free throw?*

*On December 28, 1974, Los Angeles
Lakers center, Elmore Smith, attempted
three consecutive free throws that were
air balls. It is likely that Smith received
countless calls that evening from some
Los Angeles optometrists.*

driving to the hoop between defenders so he can shoot a close-in shot or pass to a teammate.

TIP-IN — A basket made by pushing or tipping a missed shot into the goal.

AIR BALL — A missed shot that does not touch the rim, backboard or net.
- When a player on the visiting team shoots an air ball, the home crowd will respond in unison: AIR-RRRRRRRRRRRRRRRRRRRRRRRRRR BALLLLLLLLLL-LLLLLLLLLLLLLLLLLLLLL in a singsong tone.

FORCE A SHOT — A player awkwardly makes a field goal attempt while being closely GUARDED (defended) by an opponent. A player is likely to force a shot just before a period ends or before the twenty-four second clock runs out (discussed in detail later).

HOME COURT ADVANTAGE — History has shown that a team playing a game on its own court will win more often than lose.
- Home team has the crowd rooting for its players which gives them a "push" to perform well.
- Players on the home team can sleep at home instead of a hotel.
- Players on the home team are accustomed to their own court.

SHOOTAROUND — A slow-paced team practice that takes place the day of a game.
- Primary purpose is to occupy players' time during the day when there is a game at night.
- Most of the time is spent shooting.
- Players also step through some plays in preparation for the opposition.

TURNOVER — An offensive team loses possession of the ball without attempting a field goal or free throw. Here are examples:
- An opposing player steals the ball.

Oscar Robertson achieved a feat that has never been duplicated in a single season. He averaged a triple double for the entire 1961-62 season—30.8 points, 11.4 assists and 12.5 rebounds per game. That was also the first year a player averaged double figures for assists.

- Violations such as traveling or double dribble (discussed in detail later).
- An offensive foul (discussed in detail later).
- Stepping out-of-bounds while touching the ball.
- A pass that goes out-of-bounds.

HELD BALL — Players on opposing teams simultaneously have one or both hands on the basketball.

- A broadcaster will frequently say the two players are "tied up."
- At the nearest circle on the court, an official tosses the ball in the air between the two players in the same way that the game begins.

STRONG SIDE — The side of the court where an offensive player has possession of the ball.

WEAK SIDE — The side of the court opposite from where an offensive player has possession of the ball. If the ball is in the right wing, across the lane on the left side of the court is the weak side.

DOUBLE FIGURES — During a game, a player has *ten* or more points, rebounds, assists, blocked shots or steals.

- He is said to be "in double figures" for that category.
- If a broadcaster says a player is in "double figures" but does not name the statistic, it is assumed to be points.

TRIPLE DOUBLE — During a game, a player is in double figures in *three* of these categories: points, rebounds, assists, blocked shots or steals.

- If a broadcaster says a player had a triple double but does not name the statistics, it is assumed to be ten or more points, assists and rebounds. Accomplishing this feat indicates a complete player.
  - The player is not selfish because he passes the ball as proven by his assist total.
  - The player will help with the "dirty work" by trying to gain possession of missed shots as proven by his rebound total.
  - The player is skilled at scoring when given the ball as proven by his total points.

When you think of a guy getting a
lot of offensive rebounds, you picture
that player bringing his lunch pail to the
game. Retrieving offensive rebounds is
hard work (blue collar) especially when the
defenders are usually positioned between
the offensive players and the basket.

On February 11, 1982, Houston
Rockets center, Moses Malone, probably
took an oversized lunch pail to the game
that night against the Seattle Supersonics.
Malone captured 21 offensive rebounds
that night to set an NBA record that still
exists. (Offensive rebounds records have
only been kept since 1973.)

Malone would have needed
34 defensive rebounds along with
his 21 offensive rebounds to tie Wilt
Chamberlain's NBA record of 55 total
rebounds in a game. That night Malone
had only 11 defensive rebounds.

"D" — A short term for defense.
- A player might say, "we played some great 'D' tonight" which means his team played excellent defense during the game.

OFFENSIVE BOARDS — Getting rebounds of a team's own missed shots.
- Frequently a broadcaster says, "they are doing a good job on the offensive boards," which means the team is getting a lot of offensive rebounds.
- Success on the offensive boards gives a team HIGH PERCENTAGE SHOTS because many offensive rebounds are captured near the basket. The shorter the distance to the basket, the better chance a field goal attempt will be successful.

DEFENSIVE BOARDS — Getting rebounds of an opponent's missed shots.
- Frequently a broadcaster says, "they are doing a good job on the defensive boards," which means the team is getting a lot of defensive rebounds.
- Success on the defensive boards is a key to victory, because it limits the opponents to only one field goal attempt each time they have the ball.

SWISH — A shot that goes into the basket without touching the rim or the backboard. The name "swish" echoes the sound made as the ball drops through the net.
- A broadcaster occasionally will call it STRING MUSIC, NOTHING BUT NET or TICKLING THE TWINE.

BANK SHOT — A field goal attempt intentionally angled off the backboard.

BENCH — The players on the team who do not start the game.
- Used during the game when the STARTERS (the five players on the team who are on the court when the game begins) are:
    - Tired.
    - Injured.
    - Ineffective.

Basketball coach Chuck Daly was asked
his opinion about NBA officials.
He replied:

"I send each and every NBA official a
Christmas card every year.........in Braille."

• •

Former college coach, Abe Lemmons,
was the Henny Youngman of college
coaches with his constant one-liners.
Here is Lemmons comparing coaching to
other professions: "Just once, I'd like to
see the won-loss records of doctors right
out front where people could see them—
won ten, lost three, tied two."

- In FOUL TROUBLE (discussed in detail later).
- A team's best bench player is referred to as the SIXTH MAN.

REFEREES — The three officials who ensure that each team obeys the rules of the game.

COACHES — Direct the actions of the players on the court and can be called the "bosses" of the team.
- HEAD COACH — Primarily responsible for the team. He has assistant coaches to help him.

Most NBA games last about 2 hours and 15 minutes with over 200 points being scored. On January 6, 1951, a game took place between the old Rochester Royals and the Indianapolis Olympians that did not come close to those averages.

The game lasted nearly 4 hours and only 148 points were scored, Indianapolis winning 75-73. The teams battled through six overtimes. Because the game took place before the 24-second rule was adopted, each team constantly held the ball until it had a high percentage shot.

VIOLATIONS

Rule infractions that entitle the opposing team to gain possession of the ball out-of-bounds near where the infraction takes place.

The most common violations include:

- TWENTY-FOUR SECOND CLOCK — Once a team has possession of the basketball, it must shoot at its basket within 24 seconds or a violation will be called.

  - Clocks are attached to the top of each backboard to monitor this violation.

  - A field goal attempt must touch the rim (or go in the basket) for the 24-second clock to be reset to another 24 seconds. If the attempted shot does not touch the rim (or go in the basket), the 24-second clock continues to count down toward zero.

  - A team is considered to have possession when it holds, dribbles or passes the ball. Possession ends when:

    1. There is a shot at the basket (that touches the rim).

    2. The opponents gain possession (which starts their 24-second clock) such as by taking (STEALING) the ball away from a player on the court.

       a. The 24-second clock continues to run for the offensive team even if the opponents slap the ball away from the offensive players.

    3. There is a dead ball.

- TEN-SECOND RULE — A team that gains possession of the ball in its backcourt takes more than 10 seconds to move the ball across the midcourt line into its frontcourt.

- FIVE-SECOND RULE — A player inbounding the ball fails to release it within 5 seconds.

- THREE-SECOND RULE — An offensive player stands

In 1967, the Boston Celtics were playing the Seattle Supersonics in Vancouver, British Columbia. The court was not in the best condition and Celtic center Wayne Embry could prove it that night.

He leaped to grab a rebound of an opponent's shot and landed so hard that his left foot put a hole through the floor. While holding the ball, Embry tried to pull his foot out of the hole and finally was successful. The referee then called him for traveling.

Embry protested but referee Earl Strom came over to him and said, "If the other official had not made the traveling call, I would have called a 10-second violation."

in the lane for 3 consecutive seconds before a field goal attempt is made.

- A little-known fact is the lane extends for 4 feet outside the endline for purposes of the 3-second rule.
- The 3-second rule is not enforced when the offense has possession in its backcourt.
- The purpose of the 3-second rule is to prevent the tallest and/or most powerful players from always standing near their basket waiting for a pass from a teammate.
- The 3-second rule explains why offensive players constantly run in and out of the lane. Watch them, next game!

● TRAVELING or WALKING — A player advances with the ball without dribbling, passing or shooting.

- A ballhandler may rotate without traveling (called PIVOTING) by moving one foot while keeping the other foot, the PIVOT FOOT, on the same place on the floor.
- Before shooting or passing, the ballhandler may stop dribbling, take two steps and jump in a continuous motion and NOT be called for traveling.
- A player who jumps before passing or shooting must release the ball before either of his feet touch the floor again.
- A player who shoots an air ball may not be the next player to touch the ball.

● DOUBLE DRIBBLE — A player dribbling the basketball does one of the following:

- Bounces the ball with both hands touching the basketball at the same time.
- Bounces the ball, then voluntarily stops and once again resumes dribbling, all without giving up possession of the basketball.
  1. Double dribble is not called when a player is dribbling and the ball somehow touches another player, the original dribbler recovers the ball and then resumes dribbling.

The term "backcourt" has three different meanings in basketball:

- *A team's two guards who are on the court.*
- *The offensive team's half of the court that does not include its basket.*
- *The violation committed by the offensive team when it causes the ball to move from its frontcourt to its backcourt and one of its players touches the ball before an opponent.*

- PALMING — Carrying the basketball while dribbling by turning the palm up. Some broadcasters call this violation, "Turning it over."
- BACKCOURT — A player having possession of the ball in his frontcourt causes the ball to go to the backcourt (such as by passing it or accidentally dribbling the ball off his leg) and that player or a teammate is the first to touch the ball.
  - If a defensive player deflects the ball from the offense's frontcourt to its backcourt, an offensive player can be the first to touch the ball and no backcourt violation will be called.
  - Frequently, an offensive player in the frontcourt passes the ball to a teammate who catches the ball while in the air, jumping from the backcourt and landing in the frontcourt.
    1. Backcourt violation is called.
    2. A player in the air is treated as being where he last touched the floor. In the above example, a player in the frontcourt passed the ball to an airborne player who is still considered to be in the backcourt.
  - Backcourt is not called if the ball goes from the offensive team's frontcourt to backcourt during:
    1. An unsuccessful field goal attempt.
    2. A jump ball.
    3. A tap by a player during a rebound attempt so that a teammate can secure possession.
  - A ball is considered in the backcourt when either the ball or the ballhandler is touching some part of the backcourt.
    1. Frequently, as a player dribbles the ball from the backcourt to the frontcourt, his feet may be in the frontcourt while the ball is still in the backcourt.
    2. In the above situation, the player is still considered to be in the backcourt so no violation is called.

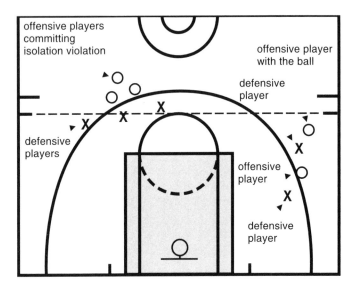

Three offensive players are above the tip of the circle on the weak side (the side of the court away from the ball) — an isolation violation.

- KICKING OR PUNCHING THE BALL — A player cannot *intentionally* kick or punch the basketball.
  - If the offense is guilty of the violation, the opposing team is given the ball at the sideline.
  - If the defense is guilty of the violation:
    1. The opposing team is given the ball at the sideline.
    2. The 24-second clock is reset to 24 seconds.
- SWINGING ELBOWS — A player may not swing his elbows (usually done after a rebound to prevent an opponent from stealing the ball) in a dangerous fashion when an opponent is nearby.
- ISOLATION or ILLEGAL OFFENSE — Three or more offensive players position themselves above the tip of the free throw circle on the weak side (with the purpose of drawing an equal number of defenders away from the action).
  - The purpose of this rule is to keep the offense from turning the game into two offensive players against two defensive players, or one offensive player against one defensive player.

*Seven-foot Wilt Chamberlain
played 1045 games in the NBA from 1959
through 1973. Wilt played the center
position where there are many opportunities to be called for a foul while rebounding or blocking shots. Not one time in his
NBA career did he foul out of a game—
an amazing accomplishment.*

● ●

*Dick Farley of the old Syracuse
Nationals had a short day's work on
March 12, 1956. In a game against the St.
Louis Hawks, Farley fouled out of the
game after only 5 minutes.*

PERSONAL FOULS

A personal foul is called when an official decides that a player is responsible for physical contact with an opposing player.

- Examples include pushing, holding or extending an arm, leg or knee into an unnatural position so that contact is made.
- A foul is usually not called when there is minimal or incidental contact.
    - An official considers whether or not the player receiving the contact was put at a disadvantage.

If a player has six personal fouls called against him in a game, he is DISQUALIFIED or FOULED OUT and can no longer participate in the game. To lessen the chance of a player's fouling out, a coach will temporarily remove a player from the game if he is in FOUL TROUBLE:

- Two personal fouls in the first quarter. He probably will not play during the rest of the quarter.
- Three personal fouls in the second quarter. He probably will not play during the rest of the half.
- Four personal fouls in the third quarter. He probably will not play during the rest of the quarter.
- Five personal fouls in the first 3 minutes of the fourth quarter. He probably will not play until the middle of the fourth quarter.

If a player is fouled in the process of shooting a two-point field goal attempt (in front of the three-point line), he is entitled to two FREE THROWS from the FREE THROW LINE or CHARITY STRIPE. If a player is fouled in the process of shooting a three-point field goal attempt (in back of the three-point line), he is entitled to three free throws.

- The process of shooting (called CONTINUATION) starts from the time a player has finished dribbling and begun the motion of attempting a field goal and ends when a player has regained his balance after releasing the ball.
    - If a player has started taking his two steps allowed before shooting, is fouled and then releases the basketball, the player is still

He heard the following announcement
by the P.A. announcer 4657 times during
the regular season in his career:

"Foul on Abdul-Jabbar."

Kareem Abdul-Jabbar played for twenty
seasons in the NBA with the Milwaukee
Bucks and the Los Angeles Lakers
from 1969 to 1989. During that period,
he had more personal fouls than
anyone else in NBA history.

Abdul-Jabbar wishes that Darryl
Dawkins had also played twenty seasons
because his career personal foul record
would surely have been broken by
Dawkins. The record for most personal
fouls in a season is held by Dawkins
with 386 in the 1983-84 season.
Dawkins is also second in the record
books with 379 personal fouls
during the previous season.

entitled to two or three free throws. The reason? He was fouled in the process of shooting.

- If a player is fouled in the process of shooting a successful field goal:
  - He is allowed only one free throw, not two or three, but does receive credit for the field goal.
  - If the fouled player makes the free throw it is called a THREE-POINT PLAY (or FOUR-POINT PLAY if fouled during a successful three-point field goal attempt).

Other situations that automatically entitle the fouled team to attempt two free throws:

- A defensive player commits a foul before the ball is inbounded.
- A player's elbow makes contact with an opposing player.
- A player is fouled when he or a teammate is between (1) the tip of the free throw circle in his backcourt and (2) his basket and has a clear path to his basket (without an opponent in between).

If a player is fouled in a situation that does not entitle him to two or three free throws (discussed above), it is called a COMMON FOUL and his team is given possession of the ball out-of-bounds.

- An example of a common foul is a defender slapping the arm of an opponent dribbling the ball in an attempt to steal it.
- PENALTY or BONUS situation or OVER THE LIMIT:
  - Starting with the fifth TEAM FOUL in a quarter, resulting in two free throws for the opposing team. Team fouls include all the personal fouls (other than offensive fouls discussed below) called against players on a team.
    1. OFFENSIVE FOUL — Called against a player on the team that has possession of the basketball.
       a. Not treated as a team foul.
         - Defensive team is awarded the ball out-of-bounds.
         - Defensive team does not shoot free throws even if the offensive team

Three General Rules to Remember Regarding Number of Fouls in the NBA

1. *If a player is guilty of 6 PERSONAL FOULS in the game, he fouls out.*

2. *After a team commits 5 or more TEAM FOULS in a quarter, the opposing team shoots two free throws.*

3. *If a team commits 2 or more TEAM FOULS in the last 2 minutes of a quarter, the opposing team shoots two free throws.*

already had four team fouls in that quarter.

   b. Is treated as a personal foul against the guilty offensive player.

   c. If called while in the process of shooting a successful field goal attempt, the points do not count.

– Starting with the fourth team foul in an overtime period, results in two free throws.

– Starting with the second team foul in the last 2 minutes of a quarter or overtime period, results in two free throws.

   1. The purpose of this rule is to prevent a team with only one or two team fouls in a period from intentionally fouling an opponent more than once at the end of a period and still not be in the bonus situation.

   2. Without this rule, imagine a team with no team fouls and less than 2 minutes left in the fourth quarter.

     a. It could foul an opposing player *four times* without putting the opponent in the bonus situation with an opportunity to shoot free throws.

     b. The opposing team would have to inbound the ball four times in a row after each common foul—not the most exciting action for fans to watch.

   3. Yes, the "two team fouls in the last two minutes of a period puts the opponents in the penalty" rule is necessary.

– If a player on a team in the bonus situation is fouled in the process of shooting a successful field goal, he is only entitled to one free throw, not two.

LOOSE BALL FOUL — No player has possession of the ball when a foul is called. The ball is "loose."

- Usually occurs while players are attempting to rebound a missed shot.
- Is treated the same as a common foul—no free throws unless in the bonus situation.

Quintin Dailey of the Chicago Bulls had an unusual request during the March 20, 1985, game against the San Antonio Spurs. He asked the team's ballboy to go to the concession stand for some pizza, nachos, popcorn and a soft drink. Dailey's food arrived at the end of the third quarter, which he proceeded to eat while sitting on the bench.

PUNCHING FOUL — Foul called when a player throws a punch at an opponent.

- Counts as a personal foul and a team foul.
- Opposing team is entitled to one free throw.
- Opposing team is awarded possession of the ball out-of-bounds at midcourt after the free throw attempt.
- The player guilty of a punching foul is EJECTED (ordered to his dressing room or to leave the building for the rest of the game) whether or not the punch actually hit an opponent.
  - A fine of up to $20,000 and suspensions from subsequent games are likely after the films of the game are reviewed by league officials.

FLAGRANT FOUL — Unnecessary and/or excessive contact committed against an opponent.

- An example of a flagrant foul is a player jumping toward the basket for a layup and an opponent hitting him across the neck with his forearm to prevent the score. That is excessive contact and a flagrant foul.
- The fouled player receives two free throws and his team is allowed to inbound the ball.
- If an official believes the flagrant foul could have caused injury or the player who fouled did not even attempt to make contact with the ball, that player can be ejected from the game.
- A player who is guilty of two flagrant fouls in a game is automatically ejected.

AWAY-FROM-THE-PLAY FOUL — During the last 2 minutes of the fourth quarter or overtime period with the offensive team having possession of the ball, a defensive player commits a foul prior to the ball's being inbounded or against a player who is not near the ball.

- Counts as a personal foul and team foul.
- Opposing team is entitled to one free throw, which can be shot by any player on the court at the time of the foul.
- Opposing team is awarded possession of the ball out-of-bounds at midcourt after the free throw attempt.
- Discourages a team behind in the score from fouling an opponent's worst free throw shooter even if he does not have the ball.

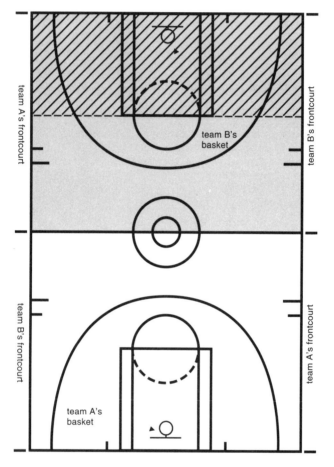

Team A's players will be called for a personal foul if: 1. They handcheck in the shaded area in their opponent's frontcourt, and the ball handler is facing the basket. 2. They handcheck the ball handler in the diagonally lined area and there is not a bend in their elbow.

- Does not apply if the player who is intentionally fouled has possession of the basketball.

CHARGING VS. BLOCKING

- Charging — An offensive foul.
    - Contact between an offensive player and a defensive player provided the *defensive player* was already set, positioned where the contact was made.
    - If a defender positions himself directly underneath the basket or if a second defender helping out positions himself up to 4 feet in front of or to the side of the basket, no offensive foul will be called.
    - Remember, if a player is guilty of an offensive foul while shooting a successful field goal, the points do not count.
- Blocking — A foul on a defensive player.
    - Contact between an offensive player and a defensive player when the *offensive player* was already positioned at the place where the contact was made.
    - If a defensive player was already at the place where contact was made with an offensive player, but he arrived AFTER the offensive player had already jumped forward in an effort to pass or shoot, blocking is called.
        1. It is nearly impossible for a shooting or passing offensive player with momentum in a certain direction while in the air to avoid a defender who suddenly steps into his path. That is why blocking, not charging, is called in this situation.

HANDCHECKING — A defender making contact using his hand or forearm, usually placing it on the ball handler's side or lower back in an effort to guard him more closely.

- A personal foul if it takes place in the offensive team's frontcourt, and the ball handler's back is not facing his basket.
    - If a defensive player handchecks the ball handler between the free throw line and the baseline, the defender must bend his arm at the elbow.

*Sometimes a technical foul is called
on someone other than a player or a
coach. For example in a game between
the Philadelphia 76ers and the New York
Knicks in 1965, the 76er trainer,
Bill Bates, cost his team a game
with a technical foul.*

*Upset with the officiating,
Bates verbally abused the officials
and then threw items at them such as
towels and water cups. Referee Norm
Drucker could not take it anymore and
called a technical foul on Bates.
The Knicks made the technical foul free
throw, which proved to be costly because
the game went into overtime
and New York won 124-122.*

TECHNICAL FOULS

Certain infractions of the rules by either the offensive team or defensive team that usually entitle the opposing team to one free throw.

- Any player on the court can be selected by his coach to shoot the technical foul free throw.
- All other players on the court must remain behind the free throw line from which the shot is taken.
- After the free throw, the ball is awarded out-of-bounds to the team that had possession of the ball when the technical foul was called.
    - If a team was fouled and before free throws were taken, a technical foul was called:
        1. The technical foul free throw is taken.
        2. Play continues with the team shooting the free throws it was awarded before the technical foul.

A common technical foul is for UNSPORTSMANLIKE CONDUCT.

- Examples include:
    - Constant complaining or criticism of an official.
    - Disrespect or resentment shown toward an official.
    - A coach entering the court without permission of an official.
    - Physical contact with an official.
    - Taunting (harassing an opponent after making a successful play against him such as scoring or blocking his shot).
- If a player or coach is guilty of two technical fouls for unsportsmanlike conduct, he is automatically ejected from the game.

Other technical fouls that are not for unsportsmanlike conduct include:

- A player deliberately hanging on the rim of the

*Former Milwaukee Bucks coach,
Del Harris, was quite irritated with
the officials on January 29, 1991, in a
game against the Denver Nuggets.
He stomped on the court to protest, running into the Nuggets' small point guard,
Michael Adams, who was dribbling the
ball with his head down. Adams bounced
off Harris and fell backwards wondering
what was going on. A technical foul
was called on Harris.*

basket except to prevent an injury to himself or another player.

- Requesting a timeout when the team has no more remaining.
- A substitute entering the court without reporting to the scorer or before an official signals him to come on the court.
- A team does not have five players on the court.

The following infractions result in a technical foul when a team commits any of them two or more times during a game. The first time a team is guilty of one of these infractions, the team receives only a warning.

- DELAY OF GAME — A player's actions interrupt the flow of the game. Examples include:
    - A member of the scoring team touches the ball after it goes through his basket.
    - A defensive player crosses the sideline or endline while an opponent is trying to inbound the ball.
    - Failure to throw the ball to an official after a violation is called.
- ILLEGAL DEFENSE — A player on defense fails to COVER (stay close to) an offensive player (called MAN-TO-MAN DEFENSE) and instead covers an area or zone (called ZONE DEFENSE).
    - Professional basketball forbids zone defenses. The rule administrators believe it is more exciting for the fans to see each offensive player being guarded by an opposing player.
    - Defensive players may leave the offensive players they are covering to join a teammate in DOUBLE TEAMING the person who has the ball.
        1. When double teaming, a player must be close enough to the player with the ball to cause a held ball.
        2. A player cannot double team an opposing player who *does not* have the ball.
            a. Therefore, two defenders cannot follow an opposing team's superstar player to prevent him from receiving a pass.

ILLEGAL DEFENSE

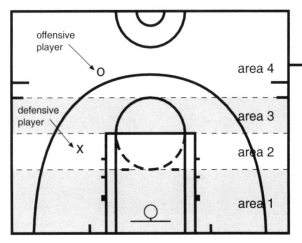

The defensive player is more than one area (as outlined by the dotted lines in the above illustration) from the offensive player he is guarding. Therefore, it is illegal defense.

• •

NOT ILLEGAL DEFENSE

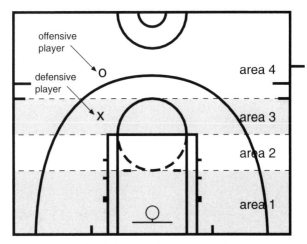

The defensive player is standing within one area of the offensive player he is guarding. Therefore, it is not illegal defense.

- Illegal defense is not called when the offense has the ball in its backcourt.
- If illegal defense is called in the last 24 seconds of a period, no warning is given if it is a team's first illegal defense infraction. The offensive team is entitled to a free throw.
    1. The purpose of this exception is to prevent teams from intentionally playing zone defenses near the end of a close game where the only consequence, if caught, would be the opposing team inbounding the ball after a warning.
- For purposes of enforcing the illegal defense rules, the markings on the court divide a team's frontcourt into four areas:
    1. From the baseline to an imaginary line that connects the two markings in the lane (6 feet below the free throw line) to each sideline.
    2. From the first imaginary line to the free throw line and extending to each sideline.
    3. From the free throw line to another imaginary line running through a small marking on each sideline and touching the tip of the free throw circle.
    4. From the third imaginary line to the midcourt line.
- Illegal defense will be called if a defender is more than one area from the opponent he is guarding.
    1. Suppose an offensive player is above the tip of the free throw circle. His defender must position himself above the free throw line (one area away).
        a. Many times during a game, a team's poorest offensive players stand above the top of the free throw circle on the weak side (away from the ball). This forces their defenders to come away from the basket and "unclog" the middle to give the remaining offensive players more room to maneuver.

ILLEGAL DEFENSE

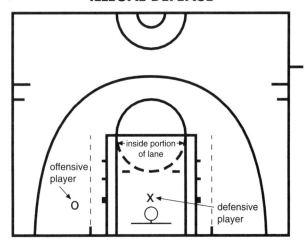

*The defensive player is in the
inside portion of the lane while the
offensive player he is guarding is
more than three feet from the lane.
Therefore, it is illegal defense.*

NOT ILLEGAL DEFENSE

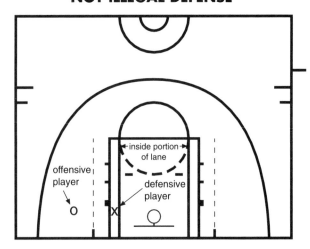

*The defensive player is not in the
inside portion of the lane while the
offensive player he is guarding is
more than three feet from the lane.
Therefore, it is not illegal defense.*

b. Remember that if three or more offensive players position themselves above the top of the free throw circle on the weak side, an isolation violation will be called on the offense.

c. If two offensive players position themselves above the top of the free throw circle on the weak side, one of the two defensive players may then occupy any area on the weak side, except that he may not enter the inside portion of the lane other than to double team the ball handler or defend an offensive player who is open because of a double team on the ball.

2. Don't forget the exception: a defender can leave "his man" to double team the player with the ball.

– Other markings on the court help officials enforce another part of the illegal defense rules. Three feet from each side of the lane is a mark connected to the baseline.

1. Illegal defense will be called if a defender is in the inside portion of the lane (marked off by two lines from the free throw line to the baseline within the lane) unless the opposing player he is guarding is within 3 feet of the lane.

a. This part of the illegal defense rules prevents a defender from covering the area near the basket instead of his opponent who is positioned on the wing.

2. Both offensive players (because of the 3-second violation) and defensive players (because of illegal defense rules) must be aware of being in the lane.

ILLEGAL DEFENSE

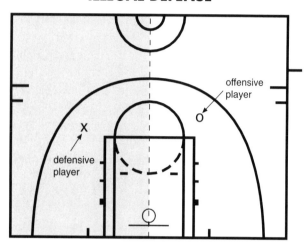

The defensive player is on the opposite half of the court from the offensive player he is guarding. Therefore, it is illegal defense.

• •

NOT ILLEGAL DEFENSE

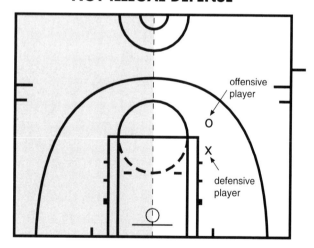

The defensive player is on the same half of the court as the offensive player he is guarding. Therefore, it is not illegal defense.

– A final part of the illegal defense rules requires a defender to be on the same side of the court as the player he is guarding.

1. An imaginary line, from the middle of the baseline to the middle of the midcourt line is used to determine if the defender is on the correct side of the court.

2. A defender may cross the imaginary line to double team the offensive player with the ball.

3. A defender may cross the imaginary line to cover an offensive player who was left unguarded because his defender went to double team the offensive player with the ball.

FREE THROW ALIGNMENT

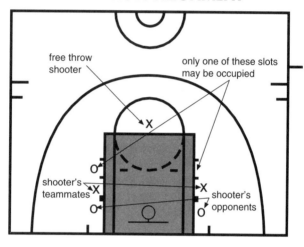

free throw shooter

only one of these slots may be occupied

shooter's teammates

shooter's opponents

FREE THROWS

The shooter stands behind the line in the free throw circle.

Once an official gives the shooter the ball, he has 10 seconds to shoot.

The four lane spaces closest to the basket must be filled in the following manner:
- Two opponents of the shooter line up across from each other in the two lane spaces closest to the basket.
- The next space on each side of the lane must be occupied by teammates of the shooter.

What about the third slots? (Here is the chance to stump the basketball enthusiasts in your life who probably are not aware of this rule.)
- Only one of those slots can be occupied by a player on the opposing team of the shooter. The other third lane space must be left unoccupied. It is not mandatory that the third slot be occupied.
- This rule allows both teams to have an equal number of players (three, including the shooter) attempting to rebound a missed shot.

All other players must stand at least 6 feet from the lane and 3 feet from the free throw circle.

If it is predetermined who gets possession of the ball after the free throw (such as after a technical foul or a flagrant foul), all players must stand behind the free throw line while the shooter attempts the free throws.
- There is no need to stand in the normal lane spaces to rebound a missed shot because one of the teams is already entitled to possession of the ball.

COMMON OFFENSIVE STRATEGIES

FAST BREAK — Racing downcourt with the ball before the opponents can set up defensively, usually resulting in an easy shot at the basket.

- Normally takes place after rebounding an opponent's missed shot.
- Players should spread out when running the fast break (called FILLING THE LANES) making it more difficult to defend, especially if the defense has fewer players downcourt.
  - It is much easier for one defender to stop two offensive players running the fast break if they are close to each other. The defender can quickly switch from one to the other.
- The key to initiating a successful fast break is a quick pass from the rebounder to a teammate heading downcourt, called an OUTLET PASS.
- Some teams run a fast break even after the opposing team scores a field goal or a free throw.

GIVE AND GO — An offensive player passes ("gives") the ball and then runs ("goes") toward the basket anticipating a return pass for an easy shot.

- The defender tends to follow the ball as it is passed, taking his attention away from the offensive player he is guarding, who passed it.
- If the offensive player gets away from his defender during the momentary lapse he is often open to receive the return pass from his teammate.

BACKDOOR — An offensive player sneaks behind the defenders toward the basket, anticipating a pass.

- ALLEY-OOP — A backdoor play when an offensive player throws the ball toward the basket where it is caught by a jumping teammate who slams it through the basket before returning to the floor.
  - The player catching the ball usually is coming from the weak side.
  - Guaranteed to draw some "oo-oo-oo-oo"s and "ahhhhhhhhhhh"s from the crowd.

PICK AND ROLL

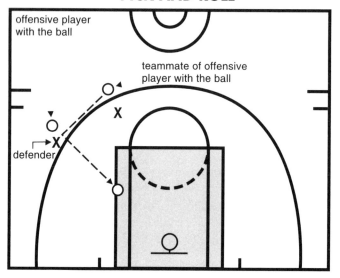

The teammate of the ballhandler sets a pick on the ballhandler's defender. Then he "rolls" toward the basket awaiting a pass for a layup.

CLEAR OUT — Three or four offensive players go to the opposite side of the court (but below the tip of the foul circle to avoid the isolation violation) giving the remaining offensive players (or player) more room to maneuver against the defense.

SCREENING or SETTING A PICK — An offensive player steps in the path of a teammate's defender so the teammate can get free for a drive or shot to the basket. Screens are extremely common, most likely occurring a few times during a team's single possession.

- A pick is frequently set for the ballhandler, but it also happens constantly away from the ball, as offensive players try to get free from defenders to receive a pass.
- If a pick is set on a defender who is stationary:
    - Contact may not be made with the defender.
    - To protect a defender unaware of the screen, the screener must not be closer than a normal step from the defender.
- If a pick is set on a defender who is moving, the screener must allow enough room so that the defender could avoid contact—usually a couple of steps.
- If a pick is set on a defender, the screener must stand still otherwise it is a MOVING PICK (or MOVING SCREEN), an offensive foul.

PICK and ROLL — After setting a pick for a teammate who has the ball, the offensive player runs or "rolls" (turns and goes) toward the basket anticipating a quick pass for an easy shot.

- Suppose offensive player A is guarded by defensive player A and offensive player B is guarded by defensive B.
    - If offensive player B sets a pick on defensive-player A, havoc is created in the defense. Who should defensive B guard? What does defensive player A do?
    - During this momentary chaos, offensive player B sneaks toward the basket awaiting a pass for an easy shot.

POSTING UP — An offensive player positions himself with his back toward the basket and just outside the lane (in

Don't be concerned if you see the shot clock turned off during a game. When a team gains possession of the ball with 24 seconds or less remaining in the period, the shot clock is turned off. Why? The period will end before the shot clock would have a chance to tick down to zero. There's a good chance that the team with possession of the ball once the shot clock is turned off will be "playing for one."

the left or right block). Once he receives the ball, he relies on his superior height, weight, quickness or jumping ability to turn toward the basket and score.

- DROP STEP — An offensive player posting up, takes a step back, just to the side of his defender behind him, before turning and driving to the basket in that direction.

HALF COURT GAME — A team emphasizes many passes, screens and post ups, using much of the allowable 24 seconds in each possession.

- A team playing a half court game does not run many fast breaks.
- A half court game slows the tempo and frustrates opposing teams that have a lot of speed.

PLAY FOR ONE — When there is less than 24 seconds remaining in a period, most teams upon gaining possession will shoot with 5 or less seconds left in the period so that:

- The offensive team will still have time to score if it rebounds a missed shot.
- The opposing team will not have an opportunity to score if it rebounds a missed shot.
- The worst that should happen is the score will stay the same as it was before a shot was attempted.

DEFENSE BOXING OUT

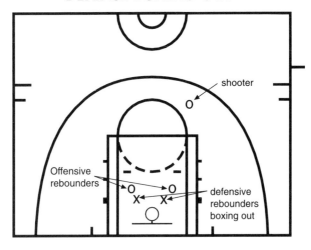

shooter

Offensive
rebounders

defensive
rebounders
boxing out

COMMON DEFENSIVE STRATEGIES

BOX OUT — While a field goal or free throw attempt is in the air, the defensive players position themselves between the basket and the opposing players, increasing the likelihood of receiving the rebound.

FULL COURT PRESS — The defense guards the offensive team in the offense's backcourt to force a turnover or use up a larger portion of the 24 seconds the offense has to shoot.

- Frequently, a full court press is used late in the game by the team that is TRAILING (losing) in the score.
- Most full court presses try to prevent the opponents from inbounding the ball or force them into making a mistake.
- HALF COURT PRESS — Similar to a full court press except the defense waits until the opponents cross the midcourt line before trying to force a turnover.

TRAP — Two or more defensive players rush to the ball-handler to prevent him from passing, shooting or dribbling, with hopes of forcing a mistake.

- Many traps occur near a sideline which acts as another defensive player.
- The downside risk of a trap is that at least one offensive player is "unguarded" which could lead to an easy basket.

SWITCH — Two defensive players exchange the offensive players that they are responsible for covering.

- Usually occurs when a defensive player is being screened by an offensive player.
- A teammate of the screened defensive player will yell "switch."
    - The screened defensive player should then guard the offensive player who is screening him. (Watch out for the pick and roll!)
    - The teammate of the screened defensive player should then cover the offensive player who is left unguarded because of the screen.

WEAK SIDE HELP

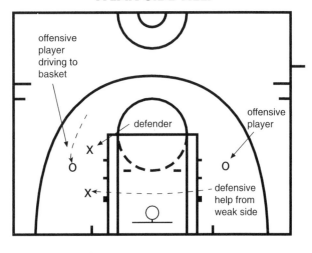

offensive player driving to basket

defender

offensive player

defensive help from weak side

WEAK SIDE HELP — If an offensive player frees himself from a defender near the basket, another defensive player on the side of the court away from the ball (weak side) comes over to prevent that offensive player from scoring.

- A team regularly giving weak side help characterizes an effective defense.
- ROTATE describes defensive players leaving an assigned opponent to cover an "unguarded" opponent.

FOUL TO GIVE — Near the end of a period when a defensive team is not in the penalty situation (less than four team fouls in the period and no team fouls in the last two minutes of the period) it may decide to intentionally foul the player with the ball (before he begins the process of shooting).

- This strategy forces the offensive team to inbound the ball, disrupting the flow.
- Having to inbound the ball and return to a position to score also consumes some precious seconds.

INTENTIONAL FOUL — Late in the game, a team trailing in the score may deliberately foul an opponent with the ball in hopes he will miss one or both free throws.

- Fouling intentionally gives a team an earlier chance to gain possession of the ball, rather than allowing the opposing team to use up most of its 24 seconds during each possession.
- Ideally, a defender should try to foul a player (with the ball) who is a poor free throw shooter.
    - The opposing team's coach may either remove his poor free throw shooters from the game, or
    - Instruct his players not to pass the ball to the poor free throw shooters.

INTENTIONAL DELAY OF GAME — Prior to an inbound play late in the game, a player on the defensive team which has not yet been warned for delay of game, will intentionally step over the baseline or sideline in front of the inbounder.

- Because it is the first time the team has been called for delay of game, only a warning is issued and the opponents once again try to inbound the ball.
- This strategy allows the defense to get a peek at the opposing team's planned setup for inbounding the ball.

KNICKS 98, BULLS 91

NEW YORK

	Min	FG M	FG A	FT M	FT A	RB O	RB T	A	PF	Pt
Olson	35	5	7	4	6	1	9	0	3	14
Smithson	28	2	6	4	4	1	4	1	5	8
Ellis	40	4	10	9	9	0	10	1	5	17
Hanson	32	5	11	1	2	0	0	4	2	11
Sanders	40	8	11	5	6	1	2	6	4	26
Wilson	8	0	0	0	0	0	0	1	2	0
Maxson	31	3	5	5	6	2	7	3	3	11
Allen	16	4	7	0	0	0	0	0	5	9
Daniel	8	0	3	2	2	0	0	0	0	2
Baker	2	0	0	0	0	0	1	0	0	0
TOTALS	240	31	60	30	35	5	33	16	29	98

Percentages: FG .517, FT .857. **3-Point Goals:** 6-13, .462 (Sanders 5-6, Allen 1-4, Daniel 0-1, Hanson 0-2). **Team Rebounds:** 8. **Blocked Shots:** 4 (Smithson 2, Maxson, Allen). **Turnovers:** 24 (Maxson 9, Olson 5, Ellis 4, Smithson, Hanson, Sanders, Daniel, Baker, Wilson). **Steals:** 17 (Hanson 5, Maxson 5, Sanders 3, Smithson 2, Ellis, Allen). **Technical fouls:** None. **Illegal defense:** None.

CHICAGO

	Min	FG M	FG A	FT M	FT A	RB O	RB T	A	PF	Pt
Davidson	33	1	2	1	2	4	6	1	5	3
McKay	41	3	8	3	4	1	3	5	3	9
Smith	27	7	19	4	4	2	5	1	3	18
Moore	42	8	21	9	12	0	1	4	2	27
Wilson	25	2	4	2	4	1	4	2	1	7
Drake	28	4	5	3	6	1	9	0	2	11
Ford	25	4	6	4	5	3	5	5	3	12
Thomas	7	1	4	2	2	1	2	0	1	4
Stevens	5	0	2	0	0	0	0	1	1	0
Walton	5	0	1	0	0	0	0	0	1	0
Mansell	2	0	0	0	0	0	1	0	1	0
TOTALS	240	30	72	28	39	13	36	19	23	91

Percentages: FG .417, FT .718. **3-Point Goals:** 3-11, .273 (Moore 2-7, Wilson 1-2, McKay 0-1, Ford 0-1). **Team Rebounds:** 10. **Blocked Shots:** 3 (McKay, Drake, Ford). **Turnovers:** 20 (Davidson 4, Smith 4, Moore 3, Wilson 3, Ford 3, McKay, Drake, Walton). **Steals:** 11 (Moore 4, McKay 2, Ford 2, Davidson, Smith, Wilson). **Technical fouls:** Ford 2:22 1st. **Illegal Defense:** 1.

New York	33	25	22	18	— 98
Chicago	31	20	18	22	— 91

Attend: 16,529. **Time:** 2:40. **Officials:** Danny Garrison, Evan Rouse, Jim Kelley.

GAME SUMMARY

A complete summary of the scoring and statistics of a basketball game. It appears in the sports page of the newspaper in addition to the narrative highlights of the game.

The following statistics are shown for the players on each team who played in the game along with team totals:

- Min (Minutes Played) — The number of minutes played.
  - Note that the minutes will always add up to 240 unless the game goes into overtime—48 minutes x 5 players on the court.
- FG M (Field Goals Made) — The number of successful shots.
- FG A (Field Goals Attempted) — The total number of shots taken.
- FT M (Free Throws Made) — The number of successful free throws.
- FT A (Free Throws Attempted) — The total number of successful free throws taken.
- RB O (Offensive Rebounds) — The number of times a player caught a teammate's missed shot (including his own).
- RB T (Total Rebounds) — The number of times a player caught a teammate's or opponent's missed shot (including his own).
  - To determine a player's defensive rebounds, subtract his offensive rebounds from his total rebounds.
- A (Assists) — The number of passes by a player that directly led to teammates' successful field goals.
- PF (Personal Fouls) — The number of personal fouls called against the player.
- Pt (Points) — The number of points scored by the player.

Includes the field goal and free throw percentages of each team.

KNICKS 98, BULLS 91

NEW YORK

	Min	FG M	FG A	FT M	FT A	RB O	RB T	A	PF	Pt
Olson	35	5	7	4	6	1	9	0	3	14
Smithson	28	2	6	4	4	1	4	1	5	8
Ellis	40	4	10	9	9	0	10	1	5	17
Hanson	32	5	11	1	2	0	0	4	2	11
Sanders	40	8	11	5	6	1	2	6	4	26
Wilson	8	0	0	0	0	0	0	1	2	0
Maxson	31	3	5	5	6	2	7	3	3	11
Allen	16	4	7	0	0	0	0	0	5	9
Daniel	8	0	3	2	2	0	0	0	0	2
Baker	2	0	0	0	0	0	1	0	0	0
TOTALS	240	31	60	30	35	5	33	16	29	98

Percentages: FG .517, FT .857. **3-Point Goals:** 6-13, .462 (Sanders 5-6, Allen 1-4, Daniel 0-1, Hanson 0-2). **Team Rebounds:** 8. **Blocked Shots:** 4 (Smithson 2, Maxson, Allen). **Turnovers:** 24 (Maxson 9, Olson 5, Ellis 4, Smithson, Hanson, Sanders, Daniel, Baker, Wilson). **Steals:** 17 (Hanson 5, Maxson 5, Sanders 3, Smithson 2, Ellis, Allen). **Technical fouls:** None. **Illegal defense:** None.

CHICAGO

	Min	FG M	FG A	FT M	FT A	RB O	RB T	A	PF	Pt
Davidson	33	1	2	1	2	4	6	1	5	3
McKay	41	3	8	3	4	1	3	5	3	9
Smith	27	7	19	4	4	2	5	1	3	18
Moore	42	8	21	9	12	0	1	4	2	27
Wilson	25	2	4	2	4	1	4	2	1	7
Drake	28	4	5	3	6	1	9	0	2	11
Ford	25	4	6	4	5	3	5	5	3	12
Thomas	7	1	4	2	2	1	2	0	1	4
Stevens	5	0	2	0	0	0	0	1	1	0
Walton	5	0	1	0	0	0	0	0	1	0
Mansell	2	0	0	0	0	0	1	0	1	0
TOTALS	240	30	72	28	39	13	36	19	23	91

Percentages: FG .417, FT .718. **3-Point Goals:** 3-11, .273 (Moore 2-7, Wilson 1-2, McKay 0-1, Ford 0-1). **Team Rebounds:** 10. **Blocked Shots:** 3 (McKay, Drake, Ford). **Turnovers:** 20 (Davidson 4, Smith 4, Moore 3, Wilson 3, Ford 3, McKay, Drake, Walton). **Steals:** 11 (Moore 4, McKay 2, Ford 2, Davidson, Smith, Wilson). **Technical fouls:** Ford 2:22 1st. **Illegal Defense:** 1.

New York	33	25	22	18 – 98
Chicago	31	20	18	22 – 91

Attend: 16,529. **Time:** 2:40. **Officials:** Danny Garrison, Evan Rouse, Jim Kelley.

Details regarding three-point field goals are shown.

- The number of three-point field goals made and attempted along with the percentage for each team is listed.
- The name of each player who attempted a three-point field goal and the number made and attempted are listed.

The number of TEAM REBOUNDS is shown.

- This is a statistic that explains how a team gained possession of the ball other than by a defensive rebound, opponent's turnover, opponent's successful field goal or free throw, or an opponent's foul.
- A common team rebound is an opponent's missed shot that goes out-of-bounds.

Includes the team totals for blocked shots, turnovers and steals.

- The player's name and his number of blocked shots, turnovers and steals are also listed.

The players, coaches or anyone else called for a technical foul including the time elapsed and the period in which it happened, are shown.

Indicates if a team was given a warning for illegal defense by either listing "None" or "1."

Includes the number of points scored by each team in the four quarters (and in each overtime period, if applicable).

- The visiting team is listed first.
- The home team is listed last.

Includes the attendance, the length of the game and the names of the three officials.

EASTERN CONFERENCE

Atlantic Division	W	L	Pct.	GB
New York	60	22	.732	–
Boston	48	34	.585	12
Philadelphia	43	39	.524	17
New Jersey	41	41	.500	19
Washington	36	46	.439	24
Miami	26	56	.317	34
Orlando	22	60	.268	38
Central Division	**W**	**L**	**Pct.**	**GB**
Chicago	57	25	.695	–
Detroit	54	28	.659	3
Atlanta	44	38	.537	13
Cleveland	43	39	.524	14
Milwaukee	42	40	.512	15
Toronto	41	41	.500	16
Indiana	39	43	.476	18
Charlotte	28	54	.341	29

WESTERN CONFERENCE

Midwest Division	W	L	Pct.	GB
Houston	55	27	.671	–
San Antonio	49	33	.598	6
Dallas	47	35	.573	8
Vancouver	38	44	.463	17
Denver	36	46	.439	19
Minnesota	19	63	.232	36
Utah	14	68	.171	41
Pacific Division	**W**	**L**	**Pct**	**GB**
L.A Lakers	62	20	.756	–
L.A. Clippers	55	27	.671	7
Golden State	51	31	.622	11
Seattle	41	41	.500	21
Phoenix	39	43	.476	23
Portland	34	48	.415	28
Sacramento	25	57	.305	37

LEAGUE STRUCTURE AND
TEAM STANDINGS

The NATIONAL BASKETBALL ASSOCIATION (NBA) is the professional major league of basketball.

The STANDINGS show the position of each team within its division based on its wins and losses.

The NBA has two conferences, with two divisions in each conference.

EASTERN CONFERENCE

WESTERN CONFERENCE

Atlantic Division
Boston Celtics
Miami Heat
New Jersey Nets
New York Knicks
Orlando Magic
Philadelphia 76ers
Washington Bullets

Midwest Division
Dallas Mavericks
Denver Nuggets
Houston Rockets
Minnesota Timberwolves
San Antonio Spurs
Utah Jazz
Vancouver Grizzlies

Central Division
Atlanta Hawks
Charlotte Hornets
Chicago Bulls
Cleveland Cavaliers
Detroit Pistons
Indiana Pacers
Milwaukee Bucks
Toronto Raptors

Pacific Division
Golden State Warriors
Los Angeles Clippers
Los Angeles Lakers
Phoenix Suns
Portland Trailblazers
Sacramento Kings
Seattle Supersonics

EASTERN CONFERENCE

Atlantic Division	W	L	Pct.	GB
New York	60	22	.732	–
Boston	48	34	.585	12
Philadelphia	43	39	.524	17
New Jersey	41	41	.500	19
Washington	36	46	.439	24
Miami	26	56	.317	34
Orlando	22	60	.268	38
Central Division	**W**	**L**	**Pct.**	**GB**
Chicago	57	25	.695	–
Detroit	54	28	.659	3
Atlanta	44	38	.537	13
Cleveland	43	39	.524	14
Milwaukee	42	40	.512	15
Toronto	41	41	.500	16
Indiana	39	43	.476	18
Charlotte	28	54	.341	29

WESTERN CONFERENCE

Midwest Division	W	L	Pct.	GB
Houston	55	27	.671	–
San Antonio	49	33	.598	6
Dallas	47	35	.573	8
Vancouver	38	44	.463	17
Denver	36	46	.439	19
Minnesota	19	63	.232	36
Utah	14	68	.171	41
Pacific Division	**W**	**L**	**Pct**	**GB**
L.A Lakers	62	20	.756	–
L.A. Clippers	55	27	.671	7
Golden State	51	31	.622	11
Seattle	41	41	.500	21
Phoenix	39	43	.476	23
Portland	34	48	.415	28
Sacramento	25	57	.305	37

Common abbreviations used in the standings:

- W (Wins) — The total wins by the team during the season.
- L (Losses) — The total losses by the team during the season.
- Pct. (Winning Percentage) — The ratio of a team's total wins to total games played.
    - The winning percentage is expressed as a 3-digit decimal. A team that has won 15 games and lost 5 has a .750 Pct. (15 games won/20 games played).
    - A team that has won and lost the same amount of games has a .500 Pct. and is commonly referred to as "at 500." For teams that do not usually win a lot of games, being "at 500" is a significant accomplishment.
- GB (Games Back) — The number of games a team needs to win (while the first-place team loses the same number) in order to tie for first place.
    - A team gains "a half game" on the first-place team when that team either wins a game or the first-place team loses a game. If the team defeats the first-place team in its division, it gains "two half games" or a full game in the standings.
    - A team loses "a half game" on the first-place team when that team either loses a game or the first-place team wins one. If the team loses a game while the first-place team in its division wins, then the team drops "two half games" or a full game in the standings.

EASTERN CONFERENCE

Atlantic Division	W	L	Pct.	GB
New York	60	22	.732	–
Boston	48	34	.585	12
Philadelphia	43	39	.524	17
New Jersey	41	41	.500	19
Washington	36	46	.439	24
Miami	26	56	.317	34
Orlando	22	60	.268	38
Central Division	W	L	Pct.	GB
Chicago	57	25	.695	–
Detroit	54	28	.659	3
Atlanta	44	38	.537	13
Cleveland	43	39	.524	14
Milwaukee	42	40	.512	15
Toronto	41	41	.500	16
Indiana	39	43	.476	18
Charlotte	28	54	.341	29

WESTERN CONFERENCE

Midwest Division	W	L	Pct.	GB
Houston	55	27	.671	–
San Antonio	49	33	.598	6
Dallas	47	35	.573	8
Vancouver	38	44	.463	17
Denver	36	46	.439	19
Minnesota	19	63	.232	36
Utah	14	68	.171	41
Pacific Division	W	L	Pct	GB
L.A Lakers	62	20	.756	–
L.A. Clippers	55	27	.671	7
Golden State	51	31	.622	11
Seattle	41	41	.500	21
Phoenix	39	43	.476	23
Portland	34	48	.415	28
Sacramento	25	57	.305	37

X = *Team qualifies for the playoffs*

• •

*In the 1968-69 season, Walt Bellamy played 88
regular season games. How can that happen when a
regular season only has 82 games? During the year
Bellamy was traded from the New York Knicks to the
Detroit Pistons. At the time of the trade the Knicks
had played 6 more games than the Pistons.*

PROFESSIONAL
BASKETBALL SEASON CYCLE

TRAINING CAMP — The four-week period during October when players get into shape, preparing for the regular season.

- Not only do teams practice among themselves, but they also play EXHIBITION or PRE-SEASON GAMES against other teams.
- During training camp, coaches decide who will be on the team (called the ROSTER) for the beginning of the regular season.

REGULAR SEASON — The 82-game schedule each team plays from November to April.

- The primary objective of each team is to finish in first place having the best winning percentage of all teams in its division, advancing to the playoffs.
- The secondary objective of each team is to have one of the top six winning percentages among the teams in its conference who did not finish in first place in their division. These teams also advance to the playoffs.
    - In the sample standings illustrated, the following teams would advance to the playoffs:
        1. Eastern Conference — New York and Chicago for winning their divisions, and Detroit, Boston, Atlanta, Philadelphia, Cleveland and Milwaukee for having the next six best winning percentages in the conference.
        2. Western Conference — Houston and Los Angeles Lakers for winning their divisions, and Los Angeles Clippers, Golden State, San Antonio, Dallas, Seattle and Phoenix for having the next six best winning percentages in the conference.

PLAYOFFS — Four rounds of play in the two months following the regular season to determine the NBA champion.

- In each conference the two division winners are

NBA playoffs

Eastern Conference				Western Conference		
First round	**Conference semifinals**	**Conference finals**	**Conference finals**	**Conference semifinals**	**First round**	
Best of five (2-2-1 Series)	Best of seven (2-2-1-1-1 Series)	Best of seven (2-2-1-1-1 Series)	Best of seven (2-2-1-1-1 Series)	Best of seven (2-2-1-1-1 Series)	Best of five (2-2-1 Series)	

1 New York
8 Milwaukee
4 Boston
5 Atlanta

2 Chicago
7 Cleveland
3 Detroit
6 Philadelphia

The **NBA** *Finals*
Best of seven
(2-3-2 format)

LA Lakers **1**
Phoenix **8**
Golden State **4**
San Antonio **5**

Houston **2**
Seattle **7**
LA Clippers **3**
Dallas **6**

Format for Playoffs based on standings illustrated

ranked 1 and 2 depending on who has the best winning percentage. The remaining six playoff teams in each conference are ranked 3 through 8, also based on winning percentage.

- Round one — In each conference, the #1 ranked team plays the #8 team, #2 plays #7, #3 plays #6 and #4 plays #5. Teams play each other in a series of games that continues until one team wins 3 games.

  - The maximum possible number of games in the first round series is 5, with one team winning 3 games, the other 2.

  - Therefore, the length of the first round of the playoffs is said to be BEST 3 OUT OF 5.

  - The minimum number of games that could be played in a best 3 out of 5 series is 3, with one team winning the first 3 games, ending the series.

- Rounds two, three and the finals are all BEST 4 OUT OF 7 SERIES.

- Regular season winning percentages determine which teams have the home court advantage (a possible extra game played on its home court) in each round of the playoffs.

  - In a best 3 out of 5 series, the first 2 games are played at the court of the team that had the better winning percentage. The third game and fourth game (if necessary, as only 3 games may be needed) are played on the other team's court. If a fifth and final game is needed, the series goes back to the court of the team with the better winning percentage.

    1. The first round may be described as a 2-2-1 series, indicating where each of the games is played, alternating between the two teams' courts.

  - In a best 4 out of 7 series, the first 2 games are played at the court of the team that had the better winning percentage. The third and fourth games are played in the other team's court. If a fifth, sixth or seventh game is needed, the site alternates back and forth between the two teams' courts.

NBA playoffs

| | Eastern Conference | | | | Western Conference | | |

First round	Conference semifinals	Conference finals		Conference finals	Conference semifinals	First round
Best of five (2-2-1 Series)	Best of seven (2-2-1-1-1 Series)	Best of seven (2-2-1-1-1 Series)	Best of seven (2-2-1-1-1 Series)	Best of seven (2-2-1-1-1 Series)	Best of five (2-2-1 Series)

1 New York
8 Milwaukee
4 Boston
5 Atlanta

2 Chicago
7 Cleveland
3 Detroit
6 Philadelphia

LA Lakers **1**
Phoenix **8**
Golden State **4**
San Antonio **5**

Houston **2**
Seattle **7**
LA Clippers **3**
Dallas **6**

The **NBA** *Finals*
Best of seven
(2-3-2 format)

Format for Playoffs based on standings illustrated

• •

*A team's success in the playoffs is
the most important way of measuring
a team's performance during the year.
From the 1972-73 to the 1978-79 seasons,
the Washington Bullets' worst regular
season record was 44-38 in 1977-78.
But more importantly, that was the only
year they won the NBA championship.*

1. The next two rounds may be described as a 2-2-1-1-1 series, indicating where each of the games is played, alternating between the two teams' courts.

2. An exception is the finals, when the first two games are played on the court of the team with the better winning percentage. The next three games (including a fifth game, if necessary) are played on the other team's court. If the sixth and seventh games are needed, they are played on the same court as the first two games.

   a. The finals may be described as a 2-3-2 series, indicating where each of the games is played, alternating between the two teams' courts.

   b. In the finals, a team with the lower winning percentage could have the home court advantage if the series only goes five games—with three games played at its court and only two at the opponents' court.

It is important to coaches that their players do well in class or they may lose their eligibility to play. Former Texas A&M head coach Shelby Metcalf said to a player who received one D and four Fs: "Son, it looks like you are spending too much time on one subject."

COLLEGE BASKETBALL RULE DIFFERENCES

A college basketball game consists of two 20-minute halves instead of the NBA's four 12-minute quarters.

Each college team is allowed six team fouls in a half before the opposing team is in the penalty situation. An NBA team is allowed four team fouls in a quarter before the penalty situation is in effect.

- On the seventh, eighth and ninth team foul in a half of a college game, if it is a common foul, the opposing team goes to the free throw line in a ONE-AND-ONE situation.

  – If the shooter misses the first free throw, the ball is live and whoever rebounds the ball is entitled to its possession.

  – If the shooter is successful on his first free throw, he earns a second attempt.

- Beginning with the tenth team foul in a half, the opposing team is entitled to two free throws on a common foul.

- Unlike the NBA, an offensive foul in a college game counts as a team foul.

  – In college basketball, when an offensive player who does not have the ball commits a foul, the opposing team shoots free throws if the bonus situation applies.

  – In the NBA, when an offensive player who does not have the ball commits a foul (other than a loose ball foul), the opposing team inbounds the ball—no free throws are taken.

- There is no college rule that automatically puts a team in the penalty situation if the opposing team commits two or more fouls in the last 2 minutes of a half, as there is in professional basketball.

- In a college game, overtime is an extension of the second half. Therefore, if a team committed six team fouls in the second half, the first team foul in overtime (seventh team foul of the half) puts the opposing team in the penalty situation.

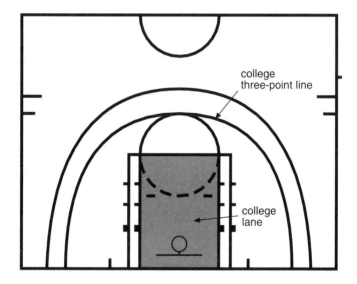

Note the college lane is narrower than the NBA lanes and the college three-point line is closer to the basket than the NBA three-point line.

– In the NBA, team fouls during the second half are ignored for purposes of the bonus situation in overtime. The fourth team foul in an overtime period puts the opponents in the bonus situation.

A player fouls out of a college game when he has five personal fouls.

- In an NBA game a player fouls out upon his sixth personal foul.
- An NBA game is 20% (48 minutes–NBA/40 minutes–college) longer than a college game, so it is consistent that an NBA player is allowed 20% (6 personal fouls–NBA/5 personal fouls–college) more personal fouls before fouling out.

Once a college team gains possession of the basketball, it has 35 seconds to shoot the ball, compared to the 24-second clock used in the NBA.

The three-point line is 19'9" from the basket in college basketball, between 2'3" and 4'0" closer than in the NBA.

The lane in college basketball is 4 feet narrower than the NBA lane.

- In fact, the width of the college lane is the same as the inner portion of the NBA lane used to determine if a defender is guilty of illegal defense.

If a college player inbounds the ball from midcourt or his frontcourt, he can throw it to a teammate in his team's backcourt without a backcourt violation being called. In the NBA, a player inbounding the ball from midcourt or his frontcourt can only throw it to the frontcourt.

The only time there is a jump ball in a college game is at the beginning of the game and to start an overtime period. Afterward, whenever there is a jump-ball situation like a held ball or at the beginning of the second half, the teams alternate taking the ball out-of-bounds.

- Near the scorer's table is an arrow that points to the team entitled to possession in the next jump-ball situation.

Bill Musselman, the intense college and former NBA coach, offered his philosophy of losing: "Defeat is worse than death because you have to live with defeat."

- The cycle starts based on which team gains control of the ball during the jump ball at the beginning of the game or overtime.
  - The team that does not gain control of the jump ball has the arrow pointing to it, indicating that team gets possession in the next jump-ball situation.
  - After the next jump ball situation, the scorer moves the arrow so it points to the other team.
- The NBA uses a different method to determine which team inbounds the ball at the beginning of the second, third and fourth periods. (Otherwise, a jump ball is used in situations like a held ball.)
  - The team that controls the jump ball at the beginning of the game inbounds the ball at the beginning of the fourth quarter.
  - The opponents get the ball at the beginning of the second and third quarters.

A technical foul in college basketball entitles the opposing team to two free throws and possession of the ball out-of-bounds. If a player is guilty of an unsportsmanlike technical foul, it also counts as a personal and team foul.

- In the NBA, a technical foul entitles the opposing team to only one free throw and the team that had possession when the technical foul was called is given the ball. An unsportsmanlike technical foul in the NBA does not affect a player's number of personal fouls or the team fouls.

College teams are allowed to play a ZONE DEFENSE. They do not have to play a man-to-man defense as required by the NBA.

When a college player charges into a defender while shooting and is called for a foul, the officials must determine if the player released the ball before making contact with the opposing player.

- If he did not release the ball before contact was made with the defender and the shot was successful, it would not count and would be treated as an offensive foul.

Long-time successful basketball coach at Indiana University, Bobby Knight has earned a reputation for being mean, aloof and quick-tempered. Former college coach, George Raveling, described Knight this way: "He's the kind of guy who would throw a beer party and lock the bathroom door."

- If he released the ball before contact was made and the shot was successful, the basket would count and a common foul would be called.
- In the NBA, it does not matter if the ball was released before or after contact with an opponent. If the offensive player is called for a foul, a successful field goal attempt does not count. End of story.

In college basketball, the clock stops in the last minute of the second half (and in any overtime period) when there is a successful field goal.

- In the NBA the clock stops after a successful field goal in the last minute of the first three quarters, but also in the last 2 minutes of the fourth quarter (and in any overtime period).

In a college basketball game, unlike the NBA, the two 20-second timeouts a team is allowed may be used at any time during the game (instead of one per half).

A college basketball team is allowed four regular timeouts during a game plus an additional timeout for each overtime period. Unused timeouts from the first 40 minutes can be used in overtime.

- If the game is being broadcast and it is guaranteed there will be three TV timeouts in each half, each team is only allowed two regular timeouts during the game. Also, each team receives three 20-second timeouts, two of which can be carried over to the second half.
  - Normally, TV timeouts are taken at the first dead ball after 4 minutes have passed.
  - When the clock shows 16:00, 12:00, 8:00, or 4:00 remaining in the half, be prepared for a TV timeout at the next dead ball.
- The NBA allows each team to take seven timeouts during a game but usually one timeout each quarter is mandatory.

NBA teams who immediately call timeout upon gaining possession during the last 2 minutes of a game can inbound the ball at midcourt—an option not available to college basketball teams.

:00.8

In the NBA, unlike college, tenths of a second must be shown on the scoreboard clock in the last minute of a period.

CLOSELY GUARDED — A violation in college basketball only, to discourage teams from constantly holding the ball. A closely guarded violation is called when:

- A player holds or dribbles the ball in his frontcourt while being guarded within six feet by an opponent, or
- A player controls the ball in his frontcourt for 5 seconds while being surrounded by teammates.

In a college game, the process of shooting (entitling the shooter 2 or 3 free throws if the field goal attempt is unsuccessful, one free throw if it is successful) begins when the player is shooting the ball.

- In the NBA, the process of shooting is called continuation, and begins when the player stops dribbling and starts his motion (including the two allowable steps) of shooting the basketball.

In college basketball, if an official believes a ballhandler was intentionally fouled by an opponent (especially if the opposing player made no effort to go after the ball) he can call an intentional foul.

- The fouled player receives two free throws and his team is awarded the ball out-of-bounds.
- College officials are hesitant to call an intentional foul unless it is extremely obvious.
- NBA rules treat an intentional foul of the ballhandler just like any other foul except if the contact was excessive (flagrant).

Unlike college basketball, the NBA requires the scoreboard clock to show tenths of a second during the last minute of each period.

- When there are just a few seconds left in the period, the tenths of a second give the players, coaches and fans a more precise indication of the time remaining.
- The NBA has helped define the length of a tenth of a second in the following situations:
  - At least three-tenths of a second (00:00.3 on the scoreboard clock) must elapse if a player receives an inbounds pass and then immediately attempts a field goal.

What Determines the End of a Period? What Determines If There is a Shot Clock Violation? The Buzzer or the Clock?

COLLEGE ---------->THE BUZZER RULES

NBA --------------> THE SCOREBOARD CLOCK SHOWING NO TIME REMAINING RULES

- At least three-tenths of a second must elapse if an inbounds pass is immediately deflected out-of-bounds.
- At least three-tenths of a second must elapse if a missed free throw is rebounded by a player who then immediately requests a timeout (because of the midcourt inbound option in the last 2 minutes of the game).
- If an alley-oop pass is caught by a leaping teammate who slams it into the basket, it counts, even if there is just one-tenth of a second (00:00.1) on the scoreboard clock when the ball is inbounded.

In college basketball and the NBA, when each half or period ends, a buzzer sounds.

- If a college player releases the ball on a field goal attempt an instant before the buzzer sounds but just after no time appeared on the scoreboard clock, the shot counts if successful. The buzzer is the determining factor as to whether a college half (or overtime period) is over.

- If an NBA player releases the ball on a field goal attempt an instant before the buzzer sounds but just after no time appeared on the scoreboard clock, the shot does not count if successful. The clock is the determining factor as to whether a period is over, not the buzzer.

- The same variance in rules between college basketball and the NBA exists with respect to the shot clock.
  - The sound of college basketball's shot clock buzzer takes precedence over the shot clock's showing "0."
  - The NBA's shot clock's showing "0" takes precedence over the shot clock buzzer.

Terms Used to Describe the Surviving Teams in the NCAA Post-Season Tournament (Also called *March Madness*)

Sweet Sixteen – *The 16 teams remaining after two rounds.*

Elite Eight – *The 8 teams remaining after three rounds.*

Final Four – *The 4 teams remaining after four rounds.*

So far, no catchy phrases have been created to describe the 32 teams surviving after the first round or the 2 remaining teams after the fifth round. Yet it warms the college fan's heart to tell anyone his team made it to the "Sweet Sixteen," let alone the Elite Eight or Final Four.

COLLEGE BASKETBALL TEAM GOALS

Initial goal — Most colleges belong to a CONFERENCE made up of a number of teams whose goal is to finish in first place in its conference.

- A few colleges are INDEPENDENTS, not affiliated with any conference.

Final goal — Win the national championship.

- Sixty-four teams are invited to a post-season tournament that determines the national champion.
  - Some teams are invited automatically because they won a tournament involving the teams in their conference.
  - A few teams are invited automatically for having the best winning percentage of games played against other teams in their conference during the regular season.
  - The remaining teams are invited based on their regular season performance as determined by the tournament's selection committee.
- After two weekends of tournament play, four teams remain: the FINAL FOUR.
- These four teams play during the third weekend, which has turned into a gigantic event.
- The team that wins six straight games in this post-season tournament becomes the national champion.

INDEX

114

BASKETBALL QUIZ #1

1. In an NBA game, if the teams are tied after 48 minutes of play, *what happens?*
   a. The game ends in a tie.
   b. The teams continue playing and the first team that scores wins.
   c. The teams play 5-minute overtime periods until one team scores more than the other in an overtime period.
   d. The teams play another four quarters.

2. If the center on the offensive team stands in the lane for 3 or more seconds awaiting a pass from his teammate, *what should happen?*
   a. The offense is called for a 3-second violation and the ball will be given out-of-bounds to the opposing team.
   b. The center must leave the game for committing a violation.
   c. The opposing team is given two free throws and afterwards will be given the ball out-of-bounds.
   d. A technical foul is called.

3. A player at which of the following positions will most likely grab the most rebounds in a game?
   a. Point Guard.
   b. Small Forward.
   c. Center.
   d. Off Guard.

4. If a player on offense shoots, and on the ball's upward path, a defender blocks the shot out-of-bounds, *what happens?*
   a. The offensive team takes the ball out-of-bounds.
   b. Goaltending is called and the offensive team receives two points.
   c. The offensive team attempts two free throws.
   d. A technical foul is called.

5. In an NBA game, if an offensive player with five personal fouls is called for a charging foul, *what happens?*

    a. The opposing team shoots two free throws if it is a penalty situation.
    b. The opposing team takes the ball out-of-bounds and the offensive player has fouled out of the game.
    c. A jump ball takes place.
    d. A technical foul is called before the offensive player is substituted.

6. During the first ten seconds of the fourth quarter, a defensive player fouls the point guard while he is dribbling. *What happens?*

    a. The point guard shoots two free throws.
    b. A jump ball takes place.
    c. The offensive team takes the ball out-of-bounds.
    d. A technical foul is called.

7. A center receives a pass from his off guard and shoots the ball successfully through the basket even though he was fouled by a defender while in the process of shooting. *What happens?*

    a. The basket does not count and the center is awarded two free throws.
    b. The basket does count and the center is awarded one free throw.
    c. The basket does not count and the center is awarded one free throw.
    d. The basket does count and the center is awarded two free throws.

8. In an NBA game, just before a player is about to shoot two free throws as a result of a personal foul, his own coach is assessed a technical foul for arguing with the official. *What happens next?*

    a. The opposing coach selects one of his five players on the court to shoot the technical foul free throw.
    b. If it is the second unsportsmanlike technical foul called against the coach, he is ejected from the game.

c. After the technical foul free throw, play resumes with the player shooting the two free throws resulting from the prior personal foul.

d. All of the above.

9. If a power forward on defense stays just in front of the basket even though the player he is guarding is near the sidelines, an NBA official will call illegal defense. *What happens next?*

   a. An official awards the ball out-of-bounds to the offensive team if it is the defensive team's first violation.

   b. An official awards a technical foul free throw to the offensive team if it is the defensive team's second or more violation.

   c An official awards a technical foul free throw to the offensive team if there are less then twenty-four seconds remaining in the period (even if it is the defensive team's first violation).

   d. All of the above.

10. Boston is playing at New York in the Knicks' Madison Square Garden. With five minutes and ten seconds already gone in the first quarter, Boston is called for a 24-second violation. To this point, neither Boston nor New York has called a regular timeout. *What happens next?*

    a. New York takes the ball out-of-bounds.

    b. New York is charged with a mandatory timeout.

    c. A technical foul is called on Boston.

    d. All of the above.

ANSWERS TO BASKETBALL QUIZ #1

1. (c) When teams are tied after regulation play, they continue to play 5-minute overtime periods until one team scores more than the other.

2. (a) The center is guilty of the 3-second violation and the opposing team inbounds the ball. If a teammate has attempted a shot during those 3 seconds, no violation would be called.

3. (c) A team's center usually captures more rebounds than his guards or small forwards because of the superior height and strength that is normally required of the center position. In addition, a center tends to spend more time near the basket.

4. (a) It is a legal block when a shot is touched on its upward path. Since the legally blocked ball went out-of-bounds, the offensive team inbounds it. If the ball was touched on its downward path, goaltending would have been called.

5. (b) Charging is an offensive foul, which means it is a personal foul but not a team foul. Because the offensive player now has six personal fouls, he has fouled out and must leave the game. An offensive foul is a turnover entitling the opponents to take the ball out-of-bounds.

6. (c) Because the fouled player was not in the process of shooting and his team was not in the bonus situation, his team inbounds the ball.

7. (b) A player fouled in the process of shooting a successful field goal attempt is allowed only one free throw but the basket counts. The same holds true if it were another offensive player that was fouled while his teammate was making a basket. The fouled player would only be entitled to one free throw.

8. (d) When a technical foul is called, the free throw is taken by the player designated by his coach. Afterward, play is resumed at the point when the technical foul was called. In this case, the fouled player shoots his free throws. (If the technical foul was called while a

player was dribbling the ball, then after the free throw, that player's team would inbound the ball.) If a coach or player has been called for an unsportsmanlike technical foul, he needs to be careful because if he gets another one, he must go to the dressing room or leave the building for the remainder of the game.

9. (d) If a team is called for illegal defense, the opponents shoot a technical foul free throw unless it is the team's first violation and it is not during the last twenty-four seconds of a period.

10. (b) If a regular timeout has not been called in the first five minutes of a quarter, a mandatory timeout is charged to the home team (in this case, the New York Knicks) the next time there is a dead ball. After the timeout, New York would take the ball out-of-bounds because of Boston's turnover.

BASKETBALL QUIZ #2

Pretend you are an NBA team's coach in the following situations:

1. The opposing team scored a basket, giving it a 106-104 lead with 3 seconds remaining in the game. *What would you want your team to do next?*

   a. Throw a baseball pass the full length of the court so that someone could shoot before time expired.
   b. Call your last regular timeout.
   c. Foul an opposing player to stop the clock.
   d. Call a 20-second timeout.

2. The opposing team gets possession of the ball in its frontcourt with a 107-106 lead. There are 10 seconds left in the game. Your team has three team fouls in the fourth quarter and one of them occurred in the previous minute. *What would you want your team to do next?*

   a. Foul the opposing player who has the ball.
   b. Criticize an official so a technical foul will be called, stopping the clock.
   c. Call a regular timeout.
   d. Play good defense and try for a steal or a defensive rebound.

3. Your team is losing 62-60 with 19 seconds left in the first half, and your center just rebounded an opponent's missed field goal attempt. *What would you want your team to do?*

   a. Shoot the ball with 10 seconds left.
   b. Shoot the ball with 5 seconds left.
   c. Hold the ball and not shoot it.
   d. Foul an opposing player to stop the clock.

4. Same situation as in question 3 except there are 39 seconds left in the first half. *What would you want your team to do?*

a. Shoot the ball with 30 seconds left.
b. Shoot the ball with 20 seconds left.
c. Hold the ball and not shoot it.
d. Foul an opposing player to stop the clock.

5. Your team is trailing 89-77 with 4 minutes left in the game after your shooting guard just scored a basket. *What would you want your team to do defensively?*

   a. Full court press.
   b. Half court press.
   c. Trap.
   d. Any of the above.

6. Your team is winning 104-102 with 6 seconds remaining in the game. The opposing team called timeout after rebounding your shooting guard's jumper and is ready to take the ball out-of-bounds at midcourt. Your players have had two team fouls called against them in the fourth quarter, none in the last 2 minutes. *What would you want your team to do defensively?*

   a. Foul a player as he begins the process of shooting.
   b. Foul the player who receives the inbounds pass before he begins the process of shooting.
   c. Call a regular timeout once an opposing player catches an inbounds pass.
   d. Call a 20-second timeout once an opposing player catches an inbounds pass.

7. An opposing player on the home team just made a terrific dunk shot for its first lead of the game 77-76, with 5 minutes remaining in the third quarter. The crowd noise is deafening. *What would you want your team to do?*

   a. Call a timeout.
   b. Shoot a three-point field goal attempt.
   c. Hold the ball in your backcourt for 15 seconds to quiet the crowd.
   d. Any of the above.

8. The opposing team's superstar center has just been called for his fifth personal foul with 11 minutes left in a tie game. His coach leaves him in the game. *What would you instruct your team to do offensively?*

 a. Shoot a three-point field goal attempt.
 b. Pass the ball to your center who will try to DRAW A FOUL from the opposing center.
 c. Have your power forward set a pick on the defensive player covering your shooting guard.
 d. Position your center above the free throw circle on the weak side.

9. Your team is losing 107-104 with 5 seconds left in the game and will be inbounding the ball at midcourt. *What do you do?*

 a. Insert into the game your team's best three-point shooters.
 b. Position all of your players near the three-point line.
 c. If a teammate rebounds a missed shot, make sure he knows to throw it out to another one of your players stationed beyond the three-point line.
 d. All of the above.

10. The opposing team has just called timeout after a defensive rebound with 12 seconds left in the game. Your team is leading 116-114. Both teams are in the bonus situation. *What do you do?*

 a. Foul their ballhandler once they inbound the ball.
 b. Insert into the game your team's best defenders.
 c. Insert into the game a player that has fouled out.
 d. All of the above.

ANSWERS TO BASKETBALL QUIZ #2

1. (b) Request a regular timeout so that when play resumes, your team can inbound the ball at midcourt instead of underneath your basket.

2. (a) Because there are only 10 seconds left in the game and a team can hold the ball 24 seconds before a violation could be called, you need to quickly foul the ball-handler. Since it is the second team foul in the last 2 minutes, the opponents shoot two free throws. Your team will still have a chance to either tie or win the game depending on how many of the opponent's free throw attempts are successful.

3. (b) It is better to shoot with just 5 seconds remaining in the half so that if your player misses the shot and an opposing player rebounds it, you did not leave his team much time to try to score. If a player on your team gets the offensive rebound, he still has time for another field goal attempt before the half ends.

4. (a) By shooting with 30 seconds left, your team should have two possessions to score before the first half ends, even if the opposing team uses up its 24 seconds. (However, if your team has to hold the ball past the 30-second mark to find an easier field goal attempt, that is okay.) If your team shot with 20 seconds left and the opposing team gained possession, it would most likely play for one shot (see question 3 above).

5. (d) Losing by eight points late in the game, increases the need to force a turnover. Trapping or pressing your opponents can result in a mistake on their part.

6. (b) With only two team fouls in the quarter and none in the last 2 minutes of the quarter, your team has a foul to give before your opponents will begin shooting free throws on common fouls. Take advantage of this by fouling the player who receives the inbounds pass, but before he begins the process of shooting. Forcing your opponents to inbound the ball again will take a few seconds off the clock, giving them even less time to attempt a field goal.

7. (a) Call a timeout to quiet the crowd. After a break in the action, the home fans are usually less vocal than after an exciting dunk shot by one of its players. If your team has not yet called a regular timeout in the quarter, go ahead and call a regular timeout at this time (since you would likely be forced to call a mandatory regular timeout later in the quarter anyway). Otherwise, call for a 20-second timeout if you have not used it yet in the half.

8. (b) Your team's objective is to influence the opposing team's center to commit his sixth personal foul, causing him to foul out of the game. Therefore, get the ball in the hands of your player (most likely, your center) whom he is guarding. The likely result is a foul by the opposing center or less aggressive defense on his part to avoid a foul.

9. (d) Your only chance to keep from losing is to attempt a three-point field goal attempt to send the game into overtime. Insert your best three-point shooters into the game and instruct all players on the court to only attempt a field goal from beyond the three-point arc. A two-point field goal leaves you a point short with almost no time remaining.

10. (b) You need to emphasize defense. If you prevent the opposing team from scoring, you win the game regardless if your team scores another point. Put into the game your players who are best at playing defense.

BIBLIOGRAPHY

Bollig, Laura. *1995 NCAA Basketball Men's and Women's Rules and Interpretations*. National Collegiate Athletic Association, 1994.

Braine, Tim. *The Not-So-Great Moments in Sports*. New York: William Morrow, 1986.

Carter, Craig. *Official NBA Guide*. St. Louis: Sporting News Publishing, 1996.

Considine, Tim. *The Language of Sport*. New York: Facts On File, 1982.

Goldpaper, Sam. *How to Talk Basketball*. New York: Dembner Books, 1983.

Hill, Bob. *The Amazing Basketball Book: The First 100 Years*. Louisville: Full Court Press, 1987.

Hollander, Zander. *The Official NBA Basketball Encyclopedia*. New York: Villard Books, 1989.

Locke, Lafe. *The Name of the Game: How Sports Talk Got That Way*. White Hall: Betterway Publications, 1992.

Malkovich, Andrew. *Sports Quotations*. Jefferson: McFarland & Co., 1984.

Nash, Bruce. *The Sports Hall of Shame*. New York: Pocket Books, 1987.

Nash Bruce. *Believe it or Else: Basketball Edition*. New York: Dell Publishing, 1992.

Peterson, Robert. *Cages to Jump Shots: Pro Basketball's Early Years*. New York: Oxford University Press, 1992.

Postman, Andrew. *The Ultimate Book of Sports Lists*. New York: Bantam Books, 1990.

COLLEGE BASKETBALL
National Champions

1939 Oregon	1969 UCLA
1940 Indiana	1970 UCLA
1941 Wisconsin	1971 UCLA
1942 Stanford	1972 UCLA
1943 Wyoming	1973 UCLA
1944 Utah	1974 N.C. State
1945 Oklahoma A&M	1975 UCLA
1946 Oklahoma A&M	1976 Indiana
1947 Holy Cross	1977 Marquette
1948 Kentucky	1978 Kentucky
1949 Kentucky	1979 Michigan St.
1950 CCNY	1980 Louisville
1951 Kentucky	1981 Indiana
1952 Kansas	1982 North Carolina
1953 Indiana	1983 N.C. State
1954 La Salle	1984 Georgetown
1955 San Francisco	1985 Villanova
1956 San Francisco	1986 Louisville
1957 North Carolina	1987 Indiana
1958 Kentucky	1988 Kansas
1959 California	1989 Michigan
1960 Ohio State	1990 UNLV
1961 Cincinnati	1991 Duke
1962 Cincinnati	1992 Duke
1963 Loyola-IL	1993 North Carolina
1964 UCLA	1994 Arkansas
1965 UCLA	1995 UCLA
1966 Texas Western	1996 Kentucky
1967 UCLA	1997 Arizona
1968 UCLA	

NATIONAL BASKETBALL ASSOCIATION
Finals Champions

1947 Phila. Warriors	1973 New York Knicks
1948 Baltimore Bullets	1974 Boston Celtics
1949 Minneapolis Lakers	1975 Golden St. Warriors
1950 Minneapolis Lakers	1976 Boston Celtics
1951 Rochester Royals	1977 Portland Trailblazers
1952 Minneapolis Lakers	1978 Washington Bullets
1953 Minneapolis Lakers	1979 Seattle Supersonics
1954 Minneapolis Lakers	1980 Los Angeles Lakers
1955 Syracuse Nationals	1981 Boston Celtics
1956 Phila. Warriors	1982 Los Angeles Lakers
1957 Boston Celtics	1983 Philadelphia 76ers
1958 St. Louis Hawks	1984 Boston Celtics
1959 Boston Celtics	1985 Los Angeles Lakers
1960 Boston Celtics	1986 Boston Celtics
1961 Boston Celtics	1987 Los Angeles Lakers
1962 Boston Celtics	1988 Los Angeles Lakers
1963 Boston Celtics	1989 Detroit Pistons
1964 Boston Celtics	1990 Detroit Pistons
1965 Boston Celtics	1991 Chicago Bulls
1966 Boston Celtics	1992 Chicago Bulls
1967 Philadelphia 76ers	1993 Chicago Bulls
1968 Boston Celtics	1994 Houston Rockets
1969 Boston Celtics	1995 Houston Rockets
1970 New York Knicks	1996 Chicago Bulls
1971 Milwaukee Bucks	1997 Chicago Bulls
1972 Los Angeles Lakers	